# TRANSFORMING

# THE POVERTY OF AFFLUENCE

## PREPARING THE AFFLUENT POOR FOR LEADERSHIP IN THE RENEWAL OF THE WORLD

*Out of a Hermit's Hear*t

**Volume One**

Mother Teresa introducing Fr. Tracy as her choice as Rector of a proposed International Seminary. Subsequently, on October 27, 1993. Fr. Tracy was invited to concelebrate a private Mass with the Holy Father. Afterward he was received with Cor Christi members in the Pope's library. Father presented the Holy Father with a document describing the purpose of the Cor Christi Trinitatis Institute. The Holy Father said: "Do this work for the Church."

# TRANSFORMING
# THE POVERTY OF AFFLUENCE

## PREPARING THE AFFLUENT POOR FOR LEADERSHIP IN THE RENEWAL OF THE WORLD

*Out of a Hermit's Heart*

**Volume One**

Rev. Monsignor George E. Tracy, Ph.D.
Diocese of Portland, Maine
Director of the Cor Christi Trinitatis Institute

COR CHRISTI MEDIA AND

St. Bede's Publications
Petersham, Mass

Cor Christi Media
11 Bangor Mall Blvd. Suite D373
Bangor, ME 94401
      and
St. Bede's Publications
P.O.Box 545
271 North Main Street
Petersham, MA 01366-0545

PRINTED IN THE UNITED STATES OF AMERICA

Nihil Obstat     Rev. Matthew L. Lamb, STL (Gregorianum), Dr. Theol. (State
                      Univ. of Münster); Censor Deputatus

Imprimatur     Most Reverend Joseph Gerry, O.S.B.
                      Bishop of Portland, Maine
                      December 8, 1998

The *nihil obstat* and the *imprimatur* are official declarations that a book is free from
doctrinal and moral error. They do not imply that those granting the *nihil obstat*
and *imprimatur* agree with the contents, opinions, or views expressed.

Includes index.
ISBN 1-879007-37-1(sc)
ISBN 1-879007-39-8 (hc)
1.Tracy, George E.. 2.Transforming the Poverty of Affluence. 3.Eucharistic Spirituality. 4.
Eucharistic Theology. 5.Autobiography - George Tracy. 6.Tracy, George. Autobiography.

FIRST EDITION

# DEDICATION

To Our Lord Jesus Christ
and Mary, Our Mother,
through whose heart
we are taken into the heart of her Son,

to
Our Holy Father, John Paul II
Vicar of Christ and Bishop of Rome,

to
Mother Teresa, M.C.
through whose intercession I became confirmed
in my call to the priesthood,

and
to  the Cistercian Community of St. Joseph's Abbey
Spencer, Massachusetts

**MISSIONARIES OF CHARITY**

54A A.J.C. Bose Road, Calcutta 700 016
4 January 1994
"As long as you did it to one of these My least brethren. You did it to Me"

Dear Father George,

The Cor Christi Institute is a beautiful gift of God to the Church. Use it to bring about conversion, through your retreats in the hearts of the people so they can live a life of intimacy in love with Jesus and Mary.

This beautiful work given to you by Jesus, here in Calcutta where you found your call to be His priest in the spirit and charism of the Missionaries of Charity, is a true gift of God.

Father George, go to all the spiritually poor. Those who suffer from spiritual poverty are those for whom Christ in the distressing disguise of the poor is often hidden from view in the affluence of modern society.

Please, Father, give your retreats to priests and religious as well as to the laity. The renewal of the priesthood is most important. Only through holy priests will we have a holy people. Form priests and laity to work with you and live as Jesus did in Nazareth with Mary and Joseph. He lived there for thirty years in simplicity and poverty.

Give your life as a victim priest to Jesus for the Church. Be one with the Holy Father, and always one with the Fathers, Brothers, and Sisters of the Missionaries of Charity. We will always be a home for you.

God bless you
M. Teresa mc

Photocopy of the Autograph of a Letter of Mother Teresa of Calcutta

Text of Mother Teresa's letter:
Missionaries of Charity  54A  A.J.C. Bose Road, Calcutta 700 016
4 January 1994
"As long as you did it to one of these My least brethren, you did it to Me."
Dear Father George,

The Cor Christi Institute is a beautiful gift of God to the Church. Use it to bring about conversion, through your retreats, in the hearts of the people so they can live a life of intimacy in love with Jesus and Mary.

This beautiful work given to you by Jesus, here in Calcutta where you found your call to be His priest in the spirit and charism of the Missionaries of Charity, is a true gift of God.

Father George, go to all the spiritually poor. Those who suffer from spiritual poverty are those for whom Christ in the distressing disguise of the poor is often hidden from view in the affluence of modern society.

Please, Father, give your retreats to priests and religious as well as to the laity. The renewal of the priesthood is most important. Only through holy priests will we have a holy people. Form priests and laity to work with you and live as Jesus did in Nazareth with Mary and Joseph. He lived there for thirty years in simplicity and poverty.

Give your life as a victim priest to Jesus for the Church. Be one with the Holy Father, and always one with the Fathers, Brothers, and Sisters of the Missionaries of Charity. We will always be a home for you.

God bless you,

[signed] M. Teresa mc

### The Roman Catholic Archbishop of Manila
121 Arzobispo Street, Intramuros
P.O. Box 132
Manila, Philippines

# MESSAGE

A truly amazing initiative, an inspired movement of the Spirit! This is how I can capture my elation as I read ***Transforming the Poverty of Affluence*** by Rev. Fr. George E. Tracy. No doubt, in every person's life, we can see the dynamic and consoling presence of God. This is much evident especially if we have the eyes of faith and the heart of trust. God points to a direction that we must tread, to a life we must live. Fr. Tracy saw the direction, heeded the call, and is now sharing the fruits of his docility to the will of God.

As we eagerly turn our gaze to the Great Jubilee of the Year 2000, we are asked by the Holy Father to broaden our horizons so that we may truly envision ourselves in pilgrimage to the Father's home. When we reflect, pray and share the beauty of life and the goodness of God, we are indeed broadening our horizons. And by means of this, we can truly become humble vehicles of renewal just like the members of **Cor Christi Trinitatis** and the people whose lives they have touched.

May this endeavor serve as a catalyst in bringing about the love of Christ in each person's heart, especially to the heart of leaders. May God keep us always in love, like the heart of Jesus!

*+ Jaime Card. Sin*
**+ JAIME CARDINAL L. SIN, D.D.**
Archbishop of Manila

**Photocopy of the Autograph of a Letter of H. E. Jaime Cardinal L. Sin, Archbishop of Manila**

Text of Letter of Cardinal Sin:
> The Roman Catholic Archdiocese of Manila
> 121 Arzobispo Street, Intramuros
> P.O. Box 132
> Manila, Philippines

## MESSAGE

A truly amazing initiative, an inspired movement of the Spirit! This is how I can capture my elation as I read *Transforming the Poverty of Affluence* by Rev. Fr. George E. Tracy. No doubt, in every person's life, we can see the dynamic and consoling presence of God. This is much evident especially if we have the eyes of faith and the heart of trust. God points to a direction that we must tread, to a life we must live. Fr. Tracy saw the direction, heeded the call, and is now sharing the fruits of his docility to the will of God.

As we eagerly turn our gaze to the Great Jubilee of the Year 2000, we are asked by the Holy Father to broaden our horizons so that we may truly envision ourselves in pilgrimage to the Father's house. When we reflect, pray and share the beauty of life and the goodness of God, we are indeed broadening our horizons. And by means of this, we can truly become humble vehicles of renewal just like the members of **Cor Christi Trinitatis** and the people whose lives they have touched.

May this endeavor serve as a catalyst in bringing about the love of Christ in each person's heart, especially to the heart of leaders. May God keep us always in love, like the heart of Jesus!

> [signed] + Jaime Cardinal L. Sin, D.D.
> ·Archbishop of Manila

# CONTENTS

## PART I
## NOVITIATE
## FINDING MY PLACE IN THE CHURCH

## PART II
## DIALOGUES

## PART III

# THE COR CHRISTI PRAYER

Oh, Lord, we are Yours.
Keep us pure of mind,
of body,
of heart.
Never let us embarrass the Church.
Keep us humble.
Keep us small.
Never let us be important at all.
May we be Your heart at work
in Your world,
Serving You, no matter what the cost.

Amen

# ACKNOWLEDGMENTS

I wish to give thanks to those who have, in their love, sacrificed many hours, some over many years, so that this book would become a reality.

Thanks to the Cistercian Order of Strict Observance, who have received me as a guest for forty years in their communities beginning in 1954 at Holy Cross Abbey, Berryville, Virginia when I was a student at Georgetown University; at Snowmass, Colorado during my years of teaching at Rockhurst College in Kansas City, Missouri; at Guimeras, an island in the Philippines, during my military chaplaincy at Subic Bay; and at St. Joseph's Abbey, Spencer, Massachusetts, my home away from home. From 1954 to this present moment, this group of men, known informally as Trappists, have planted deeply into my heart the gift of stability and eventually some humility. I believe I would not have succeeded in life without them.

To the current abbot of Assumption Abbey, Ava, Missouri, the Rt. Reverend James Connor, who in earlier days during a residency at Christ in the Desert Monastery in Abiquiu, New Mexico, helped me to discern my call to the contemplative and active life, when I was in Abiquiu to outline my doctoral dissertation. Later the Snowmass Community invited me to come for a year to test a vocation to the Order. I chose, however, to visit for one month for each of the seven years I was teaching in Kansas City. To Father Fabian of Guimeras, who met with me often in the Philippines for direction. To the abbots I have known at Spencer, to so many in the community, for the gifts I receive there which cannot be enumerated. My thanks to you will be my prayers for you. Thank you for offering me a home with you. To my spiritual director—and to Fr. Raphael Simon, O.C.S.O., who has labored to make this book read smoothly through difficult theological passages, and who consented to write the Preface, I bow in gratitude.

To the Jesuits to whom I also owe so much for what they developed in me through many years of education, and through my parish life at St. Ignatius Church in New York: a great love for excellence in life, for academic acumen, for the Holy Sacrifice of the Mass, and for prayer. The teaching I received from the late Fr. T.J. O'Callaghan, S.J. still influences my retreat work.

To his Excellency Philip Hannon, retired Archbishop of New Orleans, for his strong endorsement of our work and for awarding weekly television time on his network to a Cor Christi Trinitatis lecture series. To Rev. James Flanagan, founder of the Society of Our Lady of the Most Holy Trinity, for guiding me into a love affair with the Virgin Mary.

To Mother Teresa, M.C., who was given to me by God. She ignited the great fire in my soul that allowed me to choose to be united with Christ in the priesthood. To Peter C. Conroy, at the Catholic University of America, a colleague in Cor Christi and loyal friend, who typed the manuscript as it developed, and for his continuous encouragement to keep going.

To His Eminence Jaime Cardinal Sin, Archbishop of Manila, who offered endless hospitality during my Philippine years, strong guidance in priestly growth, and encouragement to follow Our Lord's inspirations to do this work, and who kindly gave permission to publish his letter which appears in this book. To His Excellency Joseph Gerry, O.S.B., my Ordinary in the blessed Diocese of Portland, Maine, for his prayerful guidance of my life, for the beautiful Foreword, and the Imprimatur; and to His Excellency Edward O'Leary, retired Bishop of Portland, who accepted me into the diocese for preparation for ordination.

I must also thank my late parents William E. Tracy and Laura Lynch Tracy, crucified in the midst of an affluent world, who knew the joy of the cross, and who accepted their suffering in quiet elegance and dignity. They knew the Lord and lived the Gospel. From their nourishment, the priesthood of Jesus Christ finally blossomed in this son. From them I learned that nobility is a graced state of being. True nobility must be founded on humility.

The list seems long, but these men and women have all been chosen by God in order that the straight line He wished me to live might be drawn with many fewer circles. I give thanks.

# INTRODUCTION

When, at the urging of many, the time arrived for the unlikely task of writing autobiographical chapters for this book, I sought counsel from two holy priests of the Roman Catholic Church with considerable experience in spiritual matters. I was advised by them to write. Both men are members of the Cistercian Order of Strict Observance at St. Joseph's Abbey in Spencer, Massachusetts. The first is my spiritual director, a man of wisdom whom I visit virtually monthly. The second is known in the Church not only as priest and monk but also as a medical doctor, psychiatrist, and author. He also consented to write the Preface.

Through these chapters I hope to bring readers into touch with the major developmental periods of their lives. The pattern of life the Creator arranged for me may help readers to recognize their own patterns of life. This should help them to understand that they are part of a creation much greater than themselves.

The plan our Creator has for us is initially indicated by our first understandings in early childhood. If all goes well, all subsequent understandings of the meaning of our lives will build on the earliest ones. Then we will become who we are meant to be, and God will have become our greatest teacher.

The events and experiences and places of my life indicate where my understandings were formed and unfolded. The persons and places mentioned in this review of my life are not better than those of anyone else. While many of them are marked by material affluence, such affluence may not be an advantage, as I hope this book makes clear. I have found that such affluence is frequently accompanied by an impoverishment of the spirit. Many of the persons, places, things, and experiences here recounted were given to me for the mission to which Christ was calling me. First of all, by His grace, they became a source of growth into a love affair that I never thought possible for any human person. Happiness is a product of finding God and learning to love.

# FOREWORD

The heart of the new evangelization needed in the third Christian Millennium will necessarily involve a renewed appreciation of the presence and power of the Eucharist in the life of the Church. As the Second Vatican Council taught, the Eucharist is "source and summit" (cf. Sacramentum Concilium no. 10) of the Church's life. Father George Tracy's examination of Eucharistic spirituality will assist the Church in coming to a deeper understanding of the tremendous gift that is ours as believers in the Sacrament of Christ's Body and Blood.

Father Tracy, a priest of the Diocese of Portland, is known to many around the world as a preacher of retreats and conferences. His work with Mother Teresa of Calcutta stands a witness to the unbreakable bond between active charity towards the suffering members of the mystical Body of Christ and the worship and adoration due the Eucharistic Body of Christ. It is my fervent hope that all who read this book will likewise grow in the charity which is at the same time the gift of the Spirit and the true end of this wonderful Sacrament.

May Mary, Our Lady of the Eucharist, assist us by her prayers in making her Son better known and loved by all humanity.

+Joseph J. Gerry, O.S.B.
Bishop of Portland, Maine

# PREFACE

Many unique events have occurred in this century. The United Nations has been established as a forum for discussion and decision-making. Cyberspace permits electronic communications among millions of people from all parts of the earth. Communism has proven to be a failure. Socialism and the welfare state appear to be self-defeating economies. International free market cooperation has become ascendant. World leaders who have symbolized the efforts on behalf of human dignity, like the Dalai Lama and John Paul II, have been acclaimed; international human rights conventions have been signed; and the rights of minorities have been acknowledged. The ecumenical movement seeks the unity among Christians for which Christ prayed. The Catholic Church has undergone a renewal through Vatican Council II. A Jewish state has been established on biblical terrain, while the right of Palestinians to a homeland has been recognized. The list of twentieth-century accomplishments could be extended almost indefinitely.

Nevertheless, these events, signs of an ever-renewed spring, are interlaced with problems. This century has seen more wars and devastation than the entire preceding history of mankind. Violence, brutality, and corruption enter homes, neighborhoods, countries, governments, the media, and the ministers of justice. International organized crime and terrorism flourish.

Suitable enterprises are needed to safeguard the dignity of human persons and to overcome the manifold evils that deface humanity. Human resources do not seem to suffice to bring about the peace, harmony, and unity of the peoples of the world. Divine assistance together with proportionate human means are necessary. Among such enterprises is the Cor Christ Trinitatis Institute.[1] Cor Christi, which means *the Heart of the Messiah*, has as its goal the peace and unity of mankind in the kingdom of God under the reign of the Messiah.

Father George Tracy, a David, has entered the lists against the Goliath of the forces of disintegration with a plan which is being implemented in and through Cor Christi Trinitatis. This plan will come to full flowering in the century about to make its appearance.

This book, about that plan and about Father Tracy, is for those who are concerned about their own spiritual advancement as well as for the welfare of society, and for those who seek for a more secure future in a sane world. The implementation of this plan depends on those who are in leadership positions or who are aspiring to leadership, such as active men and women, business people, diplomats, professors, government officials, officers in the armed services (active or retired), diocesan priests and seminarians, and other clergy.

While on the level of human resources this undertaking has many merits, its success depends on divine assistance and the unity of the minds and hearts of those who participate in it. The world needs unity in leaders, vision, and high moral standards in order to recover from its confusion and disillusionment. And such standards require a dedication to the One who holds all creation in His hands.

Many people in the nineteenth and twentieth centuries thought that high moral standards could be upheld without religion. This attempt has been an evident failure. The world needs the Ten Commandments. It needs them if it is not to be destroyed. It needs them if the violence which has been spreading from cities to suburbs to rural areas is to be curtailed, as Lord Rees-Mogg and James Dale Davidson argue in *The Great Reckoning*. It is the first three Commandments which give the motive power for fulfilling the remaining seven. We must love God if we are to love our neighbor and to consider all people, including our enemies, as our neighbors, to be forgiven and loved. Love and unity in that love is what alone can lift the world from its evil which betrays and demolishes the good.

Father Tracy has been prepared by Divine Providence for this undertaking. Born of parents who were unpretentious, yet who wed the wealth of finance to the wealth of the arts, he has been disciplined in both. As a layman with degrees in political science (A.B.), philosophy (M.A., Ph.L) and the philosophy of religion (Ph.D.), he has taught philosophy and theology for many years to young men and women on the college level. He has been a head master. He has trained Episcopalians for the Episcopalian diaconate as a member of the staff of

Grace Cathedral, Kansas City, an appointment made by the Episcopal Bishop of West Missouri, Bishop Arthur Vogel with the approval of the late Roman Catholic Bishop of Kansas City, Bishop Charles H. Helmsing. He participated in the official Anglican-Roman Catholic dialogue as a theological adviser to Bishop Vogel, the United States representative to the Anglican-Roman Catholic International Conference, which met alternatively in London and Rome for ten years studying the theological issues needing resolution for the reunion of the two Churches. Father Tracy received an invitation to respond to an address given at the 1976 Eucharistic Congress in Philadelphia, and an appointment as a Visiting Scholar to St. Edmunds College, Cambridge University, England, where he holds a life membership. His academic pursuits followed some years in international finance. He has traveled widely and is at home with leading families in several countries, some members of whom have joined Cor Christi.

Cor Christi aims to form priests, sisters, and laity to foster moral rectitude, justice, and peace. The term *Cor Christi,* the heart of the Messiah, should have meaning for Islam, Judaism, and Christianity. It refers to the man of sorrows of whom the seventh century B.C. prophet Isaiah spoke, who

had no form or majesty that we should look at him,
nothing in his appearance that we should desire him.
He was despised and rejected by others;
a man of suffering and acquainted with infirmity;
and as one from whom others hide their faces,
he was despised, and we held him of no account.
Surely he has borne our infirmities
and carried our diseases;
Yet we accounted him stricken, struck down by God,
and afflicted.
But he was wounded for our transgressions, crushed
for our iniquities;
Upon him was the punishment that made us whole,
and by his bruises we are healed.

All we like sheep have gone astray;
> we have turned to our own way,
> and the Lord has laid on him
> the iniquity of us all. (NRSV 53:2-6)

As in the *Imitation of Christ*, the dialogues recounted in this book represent the person of Christ speaking—instructing and directing Father Tracy and the reader. The reader will judge whether or not this is simply a literary device. The dialogues may be read as Father Tracy's meditations.

The Church is cautious about charisms, which can be simulated and can proceed from a distorted or deceived personality. Father Tracy, in my opinion, does not fall into either of these categories. They are consistent with the Scriptures, Christian tradition, and the teaching of the Church. Their themes are important for the renewal of the priesthood and the laity and are relevant to our times. They offer encouragement for the following of, and for transformation into, Christ. The dialogues have an inherent value.

Father Tracy is under the direction of a priest who has authorized him to the publish this book. His bishop, the Most Reverend Joseph Gerry, OSB, supports him and his Institute. His work has its origin in the inspiration, encouragement, and instruction of Mother Teresa of Calcutta and Cardinal Sin of Manila.

In its first chapters Father traces the development that prepared him for his mission. From a worldly point of view, Father George's family and connections are enviable, and one may be tempted to think he is boasting in his frank account of them. And when he alludes to his sufferings in childhood, one may wonder about their reality. He enjoyed model parents and exceptional material advantages.

Father George indicates that it was the very affluence of his relatives which played such a prominent part in their coldness and separations, their alcoholism and substance abuse, their divorces and suicides. Through Mother Teresa and his experiences in Calcutta, Father George discovered the blessedness of poverty, his vocation as a priest, and the work to which Christ was calling him.

Father George's severe dyslexia, not recognized until his freshman year of college, blighted his childhood. Those who are themselves afflicted, who have a sibling or child with dyslexia, attention deficit disorder, or similar handicap, know how misunderstood the failures in school of such children are, the cloud under which they live, the low self-esteem and loneliness that pervade their lives. Poor performance in these cases is attributed to indolence, lack of effort, and other character defects, and the well-intended but misguided remedies only make matters worse, until the cause of their condition is discovered, and the appropriate treatment applied. This occurs at an earlier age in the nineties than it did during Father George's childhood. The dialogues show how his wounds were healed in the wounds of Christ, the remedy that Father George's Institute and the Church offer to all of us.

Even those most sympathetic with these dialogues will recognize the obstacles to the purposes they propose. Ignorance, wickedness, and a dissonant world view are too deeply entrenched, it would seem, to permit harmony and unity to be attained. The noted historian John Tracy Ellis, in a several page interview with the *National Catholic Reporter* published in November 1978, said that there is a revolution against authority and against faith in society and in the Church— and that the leaders of a revolution never stop. He connected this revolution to affluence and said that only something that would bring America to its knees would end this revolution. In other words, according to his view as a historian, the dissension, materialism, positivism, the service and worship of false spiritual guides, gods and goddesses, and the exclusion of the truly divine from human affairs, will not be overcome by anything short of a catastrophe.

According to this reckoning, Cor Christi and similar initiatives will not become fully effective until after these catastrophes, which have already begun to occur. Such initiatives may mitigate these impending catastrophes, and evangelize the world that results from them. They will thus have their part in bringing about the triumph predicted by Our Lady of Fatima.

These dialogues presuppose a framework for the unity of hearts of all people. That framework has its origin in the Covenant given to the Jewish people, and in the promised One of whom God spoke when He said to Abraham, "In your seed all the nations of the world will be blessed." Cor Christi is dedicated to the fulfillment of this prophecy. That blessing takes place in the Eucharist, in which Jesus is offered for the welfare of all.

Many of those of different religions, as well as those without religion, realize the need to arrest the disintegration of society, while experiencing the helplessness of individual action. Technological advances have been increasingly rapid, but so has moral decline. With the failure of the "new world order," of new age spirituality, of purely natural attempts to reinvigorate society with moral values, decency, and civility, the time may come when many persons will agree to work together under divine guidance. The Epilogue speaks of this possibility. It may even become opportune for those of various religious beliefs to work together in the framework of a chastened Catholic (*Catholic* means universal) Church for the renewal of society.

That this is feasible is intimated by the worldwide approval of Mother Teresa of Calcutta and her work, attested by the universal esteem for her, the awarding of the Nobel prize, the highest honors of many countries including the United States and India, of universities, and by popular acclaim, and by her legion of Co-Workers, drawn from all faiths and from those without any faith. Mother Teresa devoted herself to all regardless of race, religion or nationality, while strictly adhering to the teachings and discipline of the Catholic Church. Father Tracy's work is born of the charism of Mother Teresa as she herself has testified.

Over the course of twenty centuries an international organization, the Catholic Church, has been established as the flower of historic Israel. Through Vatican Council II the Church has prepared to receive all the peoples who will stream to her (Isaiah 66:12 NRSV). She has offered herself as a dialogue partner for all groups and additionally, offers to unite them in a communion in which they will not lose those elements of truth and goodness, of divine inspiration and authentic tradition that they possess. She has recognized the autonomy of the social, political, and economic orders and has disavowed every form of discrimination and coercion.

The dialogues set forth a way of approach to remedying the contemporary situation in the Church and in society.

The center of the dialogues is the Eucharist, the Mass. True to its Jewish origin, the Mass recalls in its first part the service of the Word, the synagogue service centered on the Torah. The second part of the Mass, the sacrifice and communion service, is based on the Passover supper, the Seder, in which a sacrificed lamb was consumed with the drinking of wine. In the Mass wine and bread are consecrated, and the lamb is the One who was led to the slaughter without opening His mouth (Isaiah 53:7). In receiving Him, all who communicate in this sacred meal are made one in heart with His heart to the extent that they are prepared to receive this grace. The Eucharist is destined to be participated in by all peoples who, having been enlightened by faith through the revelation of the Son of God and washed in the waters of baptism, become one with each other and with the Heart of Jesus and with the Father. They are called to stand in solidarity with, and serve others, including those who remain outside their communion.

Cor Christi aims to renew the faith of the priesthood in the reality of the transformation of the host and wine into the body and blood together with the soul and divinity of Jesus Christ, brought about by the words of consecration, and to teach it to all through ordained priests, who will form the people of whom St. Peter said, "You are a chosen race, a royal priesthood, a holy nation" (1 Peter 2:9 NAB ).

The ordained priests of Cor Christi, through their membership in the Institute, will experience an ongoing deepening of a Eucharist-centered spirituality, which they will share with those they serve in the dioceses in which they are incardinated. They will be helped by the prayers and sacrifices of consecrated contemplative women who will form a second community. A third community will be composed of Catholic lay men and women who are in a position of leadership, assisted by similarly placed non-Catholics.

Cor Christi will guide leaders to the tabernacle where the Lord resides, and where their minds and hearts will be purified so that freed from self-importance and self-aggrandizement, they can praise God and serve others and the community wholeheartedly. Christ has a divine plan for the world, and it is in adoration before the Blessed Sacrament that leaders will be graced with an ordered love and the wisdom to find the solutions they seek, effectively discerned by their purified hearts, and tested by research, consultation, and trial.

The Eucharist, the grand center of the divine plan[2], contains the dying and rising of Christ. So, too, the Eucharistic spirituality of Cor Christi requires the ongoing dying to self-centeredness and sin by which the members can then with simplicity and sincerity enter into the plan of God.

The experience of the twentieth century has shown anew that all human hearts are wounded by original sin. The realization of that woundedness becomes clearer with the light of divine revelation, which also indicates that our wounds are healed in the wounds of Christ. The communion of hearts then possible will allow harmony of action. The laity are crucial to the goal of bringing about peace and unity through their ongoing conversion and communion— which is of the essence of the Eucharist—and by their action and example.

Of course such unity will require a unity of vision. Youth who undergo conversion, coming from an experience of fragmentation and alienation, are looking for unity of vision and structure in community. It is essential that the members of Cor Christi accept the spiritual authority of the Church and its authorized teaching, the faith in its fullness, as it has been presented in Vatican II and in the *Catechism of the Catholic Church*. Those not of the faith, and those of the faith who do not feel that they are called to, or fit into the category of *Members*, may assist as *Friends* of the work. This book will hopefully profit all who are seeking a civilization of love.

## NOTES

1. The English translation of *Cor Christi Trinitatis* is "Heart of Christ of the Trinity." The Cor Christi Trinitatis Institute, usually referred to hereafter as "Cor Christi," is an Institute whose Eucharistic spirituality is centered on the heart of Christ and the heart of the Trinity. The human heart of Jesus,

the Son of God, is hypostatically united to the second Person of the Trinity, who is really distinct from, yet inseparable from, the Father and the Holy Spirit. Jesus brings all who are united to His heart into the Trinity. Hence, through the heart of Christ we are united to the Father in the Holy Spirit. 2. Cardinal Joseph Ratzinger, in a talk entitled "The Eucharist as the Genesis of Mission" given at Italy's annual Eucharistic Congress in Bologna in the fall of 1997 (reported in the 1998 January issue of *Inside the Vatican*)—the theme of the Congress was the relationship of the Eucharist to Christian mission—declared: "In the Eucharist we receive the body of the Lord and thus we become one body with Him; we all receive the same body and for this reason we ourselves become 'one in Christ Jesus.' (Galatians 3:28) . . . . I, but no longer I—a new, greater I is formed, which is called the one body of the Lord, the Church. The Church is built on the Eucharist, indeed the Church *is* the Eucharist."

Fr. Raphael Simon, O.C.S.O., M.D.
St. Joseph's Abbey
Spencer, Massachusetts

# PART I
## NOVITIATE
### FINDING MY PLACE IN THE CHURCH
### I. RECEIVING THE GIFT OF THE CROSS

Though my vocabulary did not include an explicit definition of the Crucifixion when I was five years old, I did have an implicit understanding of the pain Jesus felt. Were I asked to give an example of His pain, I would have happily said, and with great conviction, "It must have been like going to school!" I hated school and managed to be asked to leave nursery school two months after matriculation. This was indeed significant for many reasons. Without knowing exactly how, I intuitively knew my will could save me from disasters. Later I was told that my first fully formed sentence was, I'll do it my 'lone.' I trusted very few people at this age. I had already begun to understand that the life of the affluent carried with it a certain manipulation of truth for one's advantage. Later in life when I confirmed this insight while watching the film "Dead Poet's Society," I thought I must have written the script in a dream and given it to someone without knowing it.

"Dead Poet's Society" is about life in an affluent American boarding school. A woman in California, known to me as Aunt Cay, took me to see the film just a few years ago. She had been sent to boarding school as a child. My experience came later. We both got the message of this exquisite yet painful film: the affluent are often taught to lie—as long as it is done with style and for one's personal and institutional advantage. I have learned that the masters can be found in the higher echelons of government, military, the judiciary, secret societies, and in cults. I believe that various philosophical systems of the nineteenth and twentieth centuries have significantly advanced the arrival of the culture of lies. We wonder why our world carries within it a process of moral disintegration.

My family on both sides favored excellent non-Catholic education for what seemed like centuries—Andover, Choate, Hotchkiss,

Rogers Hall, Dartmouth, Yale, and Harvard, as well as Bordeaux, Paris, Edinburgh, Cambridge, Fribourg, and Louvain. My parents were now facing their first major academic crisis with this youngest child! What will we do with George? I was already out on the street having definitely finished my academic life at the Patterson School, chosen as the appropriate beginning for all little Anglo-Saxon children or their look-alikes in our town.

I lasted about six weeks in the battle of wills. Miss Yeager, my teacher, asked us to draw a family car. I chose my grandfather Tracy's car, which seemed to me to be the biggest car in the world. It was often driven by John, his driver, and ridden in by my grandfather, his nurse Catherine, and those invited to be his guests. I drew his car, and though it was black, I colored it yellow. A primary feature of my work of art was the very long hood. Its distinguishing mark was that only the front door windows were transparent, and a man was driving it. All other windows were blocked off. When our drawings were reviewed I was severely criticized for drawing a car with only two windows. I hated criticism. I seemed to be constantly receiving it. It caused much pain. Miss Yeager knew my grandfather's car had many windows—for this town's world was very small.

The Patterson School was located at the northeast corner of the Federal Hill Green, across from the Congregational Church, and next to St. Joseph's Church and School. The Green was in fact a triangle. On the south, the hypotenuse of the triangle, stood my grandparents' home, located at the head of Bellevue Avenue —named I am sure after Newport's Bellevue Avenue in Rhode Island. The houses on this street were the very grandest in town and, in some cases, very grand indeed. The car in question was a visible fixture in front of what my father's family referred to as "The House," a term which infuriated my mother who always felt a certain denial of her existence by my grandmother who lived in "The House," and referred to my mother as "her." My mother was the gentlest of women in my opinion, and nearly everyone who knew her would agree.

I was dismissed from Patterson School "for being uncooperative," which stemmed from my words to Miss Yeager when she assessed the drawing of my grandfather's car. She said it was stupid to draw a car with no windows other than two in the front. I explained that the car had all its windows, but I drew the picture as I remembered it when returning one day to Bristol (Connecticut) from a New York Giants game at the Polo Grounds. My grandfather had pulled down all the shades in the back. I assured Miss Yeager that the picture was not "stupid," but that she was lacking in imagination. I had also not gained great favor at the Polo Grounds when I asked Grandpa why baseball players were not athletes. It must have been a disturbing question to a man whose picture would hang in the Cooperstown, New York Hall of Fame next to Connie Mack, due to his interests in major and minor league baseball in the United States and Canada.

I liked my grandfather. He always asked questions that brought about conversation and never put one down if one's answers were not correct. At the Polo Grounds he asked, "How do you like baseball?" I replied, "I do not like it." He and my father both looked astonished and I was asked to define my position. I said athletes should be running around, and baseball players seemed to stand around most of the time waiting for something to happen. Some time later at the Yankee Stadium, I reminded them that Babe Ruth had a fat stomach. I had determined that for me baseball was a boring sport, an opinion no doubt related to the fact that my friends always called me stupid when I failed to catch a ball. I was not taken back to a baseball game in New York until I was much older. My seat was vacated in favor of other grandchildren. I would come to love New York—with all its mixture of life. New York respects one's privacy. Bristol never did.

My early years centered around the Federal Hill Green and "The House." We lived only a short distance from my grandparents. As the challenge came to my parents to settle the education of their five-year-old delinquent son, they persuaded the Mother Superior of St. Joseph's School to accept me into first grade although it was several weeks late, and I was underage. It was a private school and, as the Mother Superior remarked to my parents, my great-grandfather underwrote the building of the beautiful and large Gothic St. Joseph's Church so my entry could not be refused. I continued to hate school.

Some years later, as an adult, as I was driving to Connecticut from the apartment in New York, I pondered the drawing of the yellow car and pulled shades. I realized that the car's drawn shades were highly symbolic of the three tragic flaws in the Tracy family and in the two principal families with whom we intermarried. Recognizing these flaws allowed me to cope as well as to suffer in ways that could not be measured. The first: it was very clear to me that money and power, in all its various extensions, were of great importance to this family. Money competed with God. That divided us all. The second: there seemed to be little intimacy among my father's siblings as well as among all their children, my cousins. Today my generation recognizes that. We rarely see each other. I doubt, except for one or two, that we even think about each other. The third: unpleasant things or the great challenges that came in family situations which were serious enough to bring us together were often dealt with by "drawing shades." Even now, people, places, and situations that are not approved can, in an instant, be relegated into non-existence forever! I lived in fear every time I went to "The House" that I might be relegated to non-existence. Fear became my motivation in pleasing people. I might be safe then.

Following the demise of my nursery school career, I renewed the academic thrust, perched in the row next to windows facing the Green—nearer to "The House" and the car. In fact the back wing of "The House" was in full view. Here at St. Joseph's, while keeping a record of the comings and goings at Bellevue Avenue, I managed to attend to the class. Within the first two months I had memorized the alphabet. When one day the teacher asked if anyone could recite the alphabet, I put my hand straight up, and began with some conviction: Z, Y, X, W, V, U, T, S, R, Q, P, O, N, M, L, K, J, I, H, G, F, E, D, C, B, A. I still do that when I am in a hurry, but before the year was over I mastered it properly—frontward.

I succeeded in completing my schooling at St. Joseph's, entering the eighth grade at the age of thirteen. I graduated from a secular secondary school at seventeen. It provided no improvement in my attitude towards school. Perhaps it is symbolic that none of the schools

I attended through age seventeen exist today. I hated everything about them without reservation except for music and choir. The dancing classes at the Hartford Golf Club, every Friday night for two years until I was fifteen, protected my sanity. I smile now when I remember them. Those evenings were known as Miss Mary Alice Andrew's Classes in Social Graces and Deportment. Joy began to enter my heart.

In the subsequent two years, the same Friday nights were dedicated to Mrs. Harrington's Junior Assemblies at the very formal Town & County Club on Woodland Street in Hartford. We were now the older crowd. Oh my! It was all very proper. I wore white gloves with my tuxedo every Friday night throughout those four years, and there were girls! Many, with their families and grandchildren, are still my friends. After these years we were "passed on," placed on the really grown-up list. Then, all through the ensuing university years, we were invited to debutante balls up and down the East Coast—to Boston, Hartford, New York, Philadelphia, Baltimore and Washington.

I think these arrangements are a sophisticated way, organized by old families, of getting us to marry one another. When I was about sixteen I was very sick with a blood disorder. Dr. Whipple gave me weekly shots. During a visit he asked me to go to Poland or Russia when it became time to marry and bring new blood into the family.

There was nothing I liked more during these years than to dance with beautiful girls at that precious time of history when young people danced in each other's arms. Girls who cultivate the seeds of becoming real women beget tenderness in men. These nights were a great balm to the pain I experienced in so many other areas of my life. I learned to be tender, and I learned to trust relationships with my male and female friends. I wanted nothing else from life than to marry a loving young lady and have ten children, and produce a family such as a family should be. I had no other answer when asked what I wanted to do after graduation from university.

Life developed from the ages of one to nineteen at a pace that was normal in many ways, painful in some, and rather fast in others. It was filled with learning experiences that, I came to understand, were certainly different from the experiences of the majority of people.

They were, however, my experiences. As I look back, I thank God for all the abnormalities, for I recognize now that in these formative years patterns were established that provided a framework for abandoning myself to the Heart of Christ. This is not possible without appreciating the cross.

The Federal Hill Green and Bristol are significant for my story. We are all placed somewhere. This location was designated in God's Providence for me. The Green sits at the center of Federal Hill, a particular part of a very old New England town. The town was first constituted in 1632 as New Cambridge and its name was later changed to Bristol. It is some eighteen miles west of Hartford on the western border of Farmington. Farmington Avenue runs from Hartford's center through West Hartford—to Farmington to Bristol, with the twists and turns and lack of logic of most New England roads. It started as a very Yankee area, but with a healthy respect, I believe, for many of the variations in life's choices. In the early 1900s Bristol began its industrial growth and it has become a small multinational city.

As I advanced from my teens into my twenties, I knew that I was compatible with people and I enjoyed my friends very much, and often in creative ways. The suffering I underwent in childhood came from the awkwardness of my conduct which was misunderstood, and led to criticisms which missed the point due to the as yet undiagnosed dyslexia, as frequently happens to children with this disability. Despite the discovery that I was not stupid and could relate to people, I had not yet met up with all the gifts needed for a complete healing of my childhood wounds.

The first in a series of gifts that eventually allowed me to love education came during my freshman year as I followed in the footsteps of a long line of Tracys to Dartmouth. As during my secondary school years when music, choir, and dance were the balm to academic pain, so too at Dartmouth, the Glee Club and the "Injunaires," a small singing group that would tour the ladies' colleges, were the saving graces of a life that was both miserable and blessed.

I was taking pre-med courses. Early on in that career I was found to be suffering in a most serious way from dyslexia. I had never heard the word and, in fairness to other educators in my life, it was not well known in the decade of the fifties. This discovery brought great relief into my life—in mind, body, and soul. With this gift of learning about dyslexia, there also came an understanding of many difficulties in my youth, principally found in piano, reading, mathematics, and catching baseballs. Perhaps I was not stupid! Maybe I would not be criticized so much anymore with criticisms to which I could not respond.

For a major part of the week I attended a clinic for dyslexia at Dartmouth. The Dartmouth Medical School seemed to be very interested in the subject. The clinic became my salvation in many ways.

Kind tutors gave me a clear message, which was implanted deeply into my consciousness. I could enjoy learning! I was told that dyslexia had nothing to do with intelligence. It was something else. I learned that with discipline and training I could reach any level of education I might desire, but it might take a little longer. I had a lifetime. I again exercised my very strong will, discovered in nursery school, and determined to get on top of the situation.

During that spring vacation I stayed with my Aunt Catherine and Uncle Taylor Gannett in Washington. I loved them both very much. We were real friends. Catherine was one of the brightest persons I have ever known. She majored in Latin at Connecticut College for Women and was an accomplished classical pianist. Uncle Taylor was educated, it seemed, everywhere—in the United States, Europe, and South America. He was in the diplomatic life of our country and served in Ecuador, Peru, Cuba, Paris and, at this time of my life, was a member of the Pan American Union in Washington. They had a home. It was very different from a "house."

My mother and I visited our Gannett cousins often. This particular visit, I am convinced, was arranged by Divine Providence. Uncle Taylor encouraged me to follow in his tradition, utilizing my talents to serve the world. When I visited my cousin Ed Seth at Georgetown University, I also stopped by the Foreign Service School and the Dean of Admissions. I applied for admission and was accepted as a transfer student from Dartmouth. The weight of the world was lifted from my shoulders as I willingly surrendered the attempt to pursue a  career in medicine. Dyslexia and endless physics and chemistry do not go together. I admire those who can understand all the formulae of physics and chemistry and mathematics—frontwards not backwards.

My chemistry professor, Dr. Fletcher Lowe, was a former class-mate of my father at Dartmouth. During one of my father's visits to the school Dad had breakfast with him. He assured my father that I would pass chemistry but demanded that Dad promise him that af-ter that I would never enter the chemistry building again. One day my physics professor closed and locked the classroom door in front of me as I arrived, barring my entry. Happily I have forgotten his name. People still ask me what I did not like about Dartmouth. My answer is always about what I did like, emphasizing my growth through my respect and love for professors Paul Zellar and Paul Sample, my professors of music and painting respectively. No matter how many doors were locked in front of me, life's refined moments and the world of fine arts provided a path to the future. Somehow I knew I could always touch God there.

I had now begun the long process that was to become a lifetime task, to understand and to master dyslexia—to know the origin of the dark side of my youth, to deal with numbers and letters, and to discern whether to use a left or right hand in sports. Today I hit a golf or tennis ball from the right and a baseball from the left, and can do both most of the time. The greatest relief was to understand why I nearly always got hit on the head trying to catch a fly ball. The glove was always a few inches off center. Now I knew the reason. Under-standing my dyslexia was as freeing as Waltz Nights in Boston.

During the ensuing years, I experienced a series of resurrections, after so many other experiences that were a sharing in the garden of Gethsemane. My advance into freedom, safeguarded by a strong will, was fueled by my profound and continuous love for nature's beauty and fine arts, which comes from generations of my mother's heri-tage. I must also give credit to the refinement of my father's family, and the positive gifts received at Federal Hill and "The House."

I was deeply influenced by the goodness, modesty, and simplicity of my parents and their Connecticut friends. My parents were blessed amidst years of clan turmoil. I never heard either of them raise their voices during my lifetime with them. They lived in a formal and dignified way, and both possessed a good sense of humor. I received their love and care, and also the cross that comes to all of us. Rose Perry also provided stability. At a very young age, she began working for my grandparents Lynch. After their death, she came to our home until she was nearly eighty.

Catherine Flynn, a registered nurse, was another stone in our foundation. She was our nurse and our friend and cared for the needs of two generations of Tracys. She is still alive, and lives with her sister Mary Riorden in Old Saybrook, Connecticut. I try to visit them whenever I can. No small gifts from God.

One of the most valuable insights of my youth occurred one spring vacation on a visit to very close friends from Farmington, Connecticut at their home in Bal Harbor on Miami Beach—a friendship which still continues. They are the Clark family with four Clark children— now in their middle years, discreetly stated. On this occasion a few friends had gathered at the Clarks. Vacation was a busy few days and activities abounded.

One night the young crowd were going off to a party. I was at a moment when my hermit's heart had the upper hand, and I decided not to go to the big party. I sat in the garden with a few of the Clark adults and friends. Mrs. Clark and I had a most intuitive friendship. She and my mother had great respect for each other as well. My father and her husband knew each other through business. I joined Mrs. Clark and one or two others in the pool. Mrs. Clark spoke to me discreetly about my staying home for the evening. She said that my ability to make my own decisions should never be compromised. That sounded like a very serious statement. So I indicated my intense desire to hear her, saying, "Speak to me." She spoke about the false values of life that can come with life-styles we both knew, she for many more years than I. She had a beautiful, insightful way of teaching, with a gentle voice, an embracing smile, a light laugh, and twinkling blue eyes. In a mixture of all these characteristics profound truths were often given to those who wanted to listen here in Florida, or in Farmington at the kitchen table, with milk and cookies, or by the fire in the library, her favorite places for teaching youth. Many of us sat with her to listen.

This night she said to me, "George, never get attached to the kind of life you see this week in Florida, or anywhere else. You have a contemplative heart, and I hope you will one day be a college professor or a headmaster of a secondary school." Little did I know I would eventually be both. She continued to say that I must treasure my interior life and stop periodically to think about the life I was watching in Bal Harbor in its various aspects. She looked me straight in the eye and said, "It's all whipped cream. One good puff and it will all disappear!" It was an invitation to me never to let the material world trap me. I have tried to carry out that advice.

Edith Adams Clark was a woman of great wisdom and joy, which I later discovered came from much suffering. She should be remembered. She was a Quaker by heritage and exemplified their simplicity of life in the midst of great wealth which never touched her adversely. She, my Mother, and Aunt Catherine planted in my soul the seeds that later in life allowed me to accept the love of Mother Teresa and pass through the conversion that I experienced in Calcutta. They all knew I needed it. Bill and David Clark remain in my private circle of friends, as my brothers. I rarely see Sally and Eleanor for geographical reasons, but their brothers keep me up-to-date. We were children "on the string" at Miss Mary Alice's dancing classes that wove many of us together for life. I wonder often if today's youth are able to form friendships in their early youth that will last for life. I hope so.

In writing this chapter I have chosen situations and individuals through whom my growth took place. From tensions and oppositions, insights burst forth that lead to our understanding of our history. We must be extremely sensitive to our oppositions and realize that they foster our self-appropriations. They are turning points, the "limit moments" referred to in *Blessed Rage for Order* by Reverend David Tracy (no relation), professor at the University of Chicago. Studying his work was indeed a turning point unifying my philosophical and theological understanding. I once told the author that the text was like a beautiful symphony—a perfect circle of harmony from beginning to end. So should be our life.

I am concerned with the question: Do we realize sufficiently how very formative our early experiences are? I really believe, along with many colleagues with whom I have taught in various universities for nearly twenty years, that our temperaments—which are so influential in our thinking, emotions, and behavior—are formed by the age of five, if not by the age of three. Dr. Agatha Sidlauskas, former Director of the Child Study Center at the University of Ottawa, who also became a great friend, held this to be true.

In order to gather into this literary portrait all the gifts I received—like so many colors that complete the painting—I must return to Bristol which, for several generations, produced an unusual number of families of significant wealth and education, considering the size of the town. It is closely related to Hartford and at the same time has the geographical blessing of a valley through which runs a river, allowing for power and industry. The New York, New Haven, and Hartford Railroad had a branch that passed through the river valley distributing freight with ease to this world. Many significant factories were developed and blazed mightily during the two world wars. A small number of families owned the factories, a few others owned the banks. My father's family became strongly identified with the Hartford insurance industry from its inception and completed the purchase of many sizable tracts of land in and beyond Bristol's limits, providing for extensive developments. These two areas of business, insurance and real estate, became synonymous with this family.

My mother's family influenced my formation when I was older. My Mother's father, John Lynch was born in the Goshen-Litchfield area and his wife, Catherine Corrigan, was from Waterbury. He is remembered for his disciplined character and brilliance as an engineer for General Motors. He invented the ballbearing.

John Lynch was born of Garrett Lynch, who was born in Lynch Castle in Galway City, Ireland. Garrett sailed to New Haven, Connecticut with a friend and crew in the early 1800s. He stayed and married a Quaker, Theresa Downs, from Litchfield. My Grandmother Lynch was born Catherine Corrigan in an Irish family that included Archbishop Michael Augustine Corrigan of New York, one of the first planners of St. Patrick's Cathedral.

I read Archbishop Corrigan's life story when I was preparing for ordination. I was impressed by his ordered life of prayer, study, and working habits, for which his biographer said he was known. I never knew him, but in my youth two of my mother's first cousins, whom I knew very well, were also priests. Father Franklin Corrigan was chaplain for the Religious of the Sacred Heart in Greenwich, Connecticut, and his brother was Father Gerald Corrigan. They were educated at Louvain and exhibited many of the characteristics of our late Archbishop relative. In my ordination I prayed to all three of them for their guidance from heaven as I joined them in the priesthood. Today the Pastor of the family's St. Joseph Church on the Federal Hill Green is a cousin of my own generation, Rev. James Leary, another Corrigan grandson.

As my grandparents Lynch died before my birth, my principal formation, until I went to Georgetown, stemmed from my father's clan—and clan it was—a strange mixture of love, embodied in my grandfather Tracy, and of coldness in a woman of strong judgment, my grandmother, born Ellen de Lacy according to her marriage certificate. Her siblings in the United States were all known, as are their offspring, as Lacey, but my grandmother treasured her French ancestry and spoke to me about it often. While she acknowledged her mother's Irish Fitzgerald heritage, it was the French de Lacy heritage she held dearest. My paternal lineage is also French, dating back to the eleventh century as de Tracy.

When I was at Cambridge as a Visiting Scholar I came to know the descendants of the family in England. Merlin Tracy, Lord Sudeley, who maintains the Tracy family genealogy, became a close friend. He invited me to come with him to view the family records and examine the enormous scroll available for viewing in London. It is established that Sir William de Tracy, one of the two knights who murdered St. Thomas Becket, Archbishop of Canterbury, is a direct ancestor. We always had a small scroll in our home telling of this event.

This knowledge became formative in my desire to help rectify the sickness of our world. I felt a responsibility to make up for the historical damage my own family had caused in the Church. I also embraced, with conviction, what I had learned from Dr. Agatha Sidlauskas at the Child Study Center, that family dysfunctionality continues through generations. It only ends when individuals in any given generation take the concrete steps to forgive those family members of their past who have chosen to hang on to it. My joy at being asked to give conferences and retreats today in the United Kingdom comes in a major way from this desire to repair, even perhaps in the smallest degree, some of the damage caused in the past not only through my own family, but also through others. We must all break whatever chains are there, and accept a new freedom.

I learned that it was essential to offer forgiveness to all persons whom I believed had injured me, if I were to break the chains of my dysfunctional history. The forgiveness had to be unqualified and carry no hanging on to a pride-filled defense of self. For me, this task even included sitting at graves in a cemetery forgiving members of my ancestry. To forgive is essential. It is intrinsic to human growth. Whether or not our forgiveness is accepted, or whether people offer us forgiveness is not important at all. It is our own personal forgiveness given to others that breaks the chains of sick dependence—on people and on their sick attitudes.

With the help of my English cousin, I have been able to trace our family through all generations from 1035 to 1997—from France through England, Wales, Scotland, and Ireland to North America.

Thomas Tracy arrived first in 1632 as part of the Berkeley Hundred in Jamestown, Virginia. Patrick arrived a little later in 1634, in Newburyport, Massachusetts. The front building of the current Newburyport Library is, in fact, his original home. Family portraits and furniture are preserved in the front parlors. Patrick's son Nathaniel became well known in early New England political life. Patrick gave him, as a marriage gift, the beautiful house still-standing in Cambridge, Massachusetts known now as the Longfellow

House, which borders the Harvard campus. The Longfellows purchased it at a later date.

In 1634 Thomas Tracy became a founder of Norwich, Connecticut. My immediate ancestors came to Bristol and to 104 Bellevue Avenue on Federal Hill Green. Both sides of my family formed a tapestry of Roman Catholic and Protestant backgrounds, as they still do today on both sides of the ocean.

My final reference to "The House" will paint a lighter side through the extraordinary rituals that took place on Sunday mornings. Whenever possible, the Tracy family gathered at 104 for dinner following Sunday Mass. The port of entry was called the "side door" where all the cars parked facing the Green. Everyone seemed to follow the path to the playroom, sometimes referred to as the den, where my magnificent grandfather sat in a huge black leather chair. He seemed always to be in a perfectly tailored navy blue suit, with vest, very heavily starched white shirt, and a tie of conservative elegance secured with a discreet diamond stick pin. His black shoes glowed like the fenders of his large black car. Grandpa was known to all his friends and business colleagues both in Connecticut and New York as W.J. To the world W.J. stood for William Joseph, but to me those initials meant "What Joy." And joy he was. His life was the ultimate of dignity, kindness, and long suffering, which gift allowed him to pacify periodic tantrums of various family members at business discussions throughout too many years of his life. Grandpa died of a massive coronary at the height of his business career. He was only sixty. Perhaps we all wore him out.

Once we were all in the den, ritual number two commenced. John O'Brien, grandpa's chauffeur, butler, and most of all his close friend and surely his confidant, would come to the den doorway. He would begin the roll call for the grandchildren to endure our weekly presentation to my grandmother in the music room.

Without ever a change, John would signal us one by one from the oldest to the youngest, in nearly military readiness, and guide us with hand on our shoulders to the music room. The room was the definition of old-world formality—piano to the right, organ to the left, and straight ahead in a group, on a couch flanked by two chairs, my grandmother and her friends, Mrs. Hawkshurst and Mrs. Cushner. They sat like protecting guards of what looked like a fire-sale from Tiffany's. Silver pots of English tea, hot water, and silver bowls of sweets were piled on a huge, elaborate silver tray centered on a coffee table and filled with endless cups and saucers, so delicate that they tested the limits of physics. We grandchildren tried to lift them without a spill.

Upon arrival at the music room door, John would say. "Your grand-son, George"—or whoever it might be. He would hold my left shoulder with the grip of his right hand, and then releasing me, disappear.

As we were never in the music room with any of our cousins, I can only describe the event as an invitee in my turn. Immediately my grandmother would issue a "Good morning." Mrs. Hawkshurst would then lift to her eyes her lorgnette, which looked like little windows on a silver stick attached to her neck by a chain, and remark that I had new knickers. I would assure her I had the same ones on as last week. My comment seemed to pass her ears, and Mrs. Cushner, on key, would invite me to move closer to the fire-sale for tea. My grand-mother would indicate the needlepointed bench on which we sat in turn. She would then gesture to Mary, who stood at the organ in bent attention, to pour tea for George.

Mary spent her lifetime serving the family in the kitchen, under the command of Bertha, a superb cook, who produced a flow of food that seemed never to run out. Mary baked the pies. She was also in charge of Sunday morning tea. She would pour the tea and add two lumps of sugar with a silver-pronged affair with eagle claws that looked rather lethal to my youthful eyes. Then she would add milk and, with hand trembling due to her age, she would pass the cup and saucer to the recipient. Conversation would take place until the tea was con-sumed and the next grandchild arrived. Thus my grandmother! I am happy to report that later in life I did discover her heart. I was also grateful for her early training when I was at Georgetown preparing for a life in the diplomatic corps. I was often at embassy affairs where, now and then, tea would be served, reminding me of Sundays at 104 Bellevue Avenue. I was well prepared for life in Washington.

Mother's family was wholly other than my father's clan. The Tracys were an organization. They still are not a family. This is a great sadness for me today as I watch the subsequent generations enjoy increased wealth and exhibit what appears to be even greater loss of love and unity. Though very different in approach to life, both sides were made up of very good and refined people. Mother's family was, as mentioned earlier, also from a Connecticut foundation in Litchfield County. Some are still there, as are also part of Dad's family.

The emphasis of the Lynch family was on fine arts, literature, graduate education, and summers on the coast of Maine. Though the Tracy family was not totally divorced from these pursuits, having, for example, regular seats at the Metropolitan Opera in New York from its inception, the emphasis was definitely on education in order to be successful in business. On mother's side the emphasis seemed always to be on education for living a good life—virtue came first. Her family was intermarried with established Protestant families throughout New England. It is from them that I believe I have most of my genes.

I spent my first summer in Maine when I was five years old at the wonderful summer home of my Aunt Mae and Uncle Dan Sylvester. They lived in a truly beautiful ancient Maine cape house on a hill with a long front lawn to the sea. Behind the house a meadow filled with daisies was enclosed by a pine forest. I now realize that the reason I liked so much to romp among those daisies was because of the protection of those pine trees. I felt very safe. The beauty of creation was all around me. As years went by, especially after Grandpa Tracy's death, I never really felt safe spiritually or emotionally in the Tracy clan. I always felt safe with most of mother's family.

In Maine I loved to play alone. I was filled with the companionship of nature, pine trees, leaves, daises, beach roses, the breeze, and the ripples of water. The daisy meadow locked in by those pines was my space, and I was at peace. I am still in love with Maine and am at peace there. As decades have flowed by, Maine has remained a constant. How can one be shamed by nature? The security of being in love with nature provided a base for me to fall, slowly and confidently, in love with people, and Jesus. Eventually there were no more possibilities of being shamed.

After Boothbay summer visits for some years at Uncle Dan's, when I was young, our summers focused more on a home on a Connecticut lake, and at Black Point on Long Island Sound. I eventually returned to full summers in Maine to a rambling white farmhouse, again on a hill, with ten acres of front lawn reaching again to the sea, near Damariscotta. The pine trees were there but were scattered. The area was very beautiful, but somehow lacked the feeling of intimacy.

The third and final summer home was on the island of Islesboro centered in Penobscot Bay, on "the Mill Creek." It was intimate. I am not certain what I mean by that, but it has to do with the heart and nature. Our intimate home on Islesboro was again situated on a hill. The house was a small jewel stuffed with family rugs and antique American furniture. The Islesboro house, now that I think of it, must have been arranged by God, for the back of the property was again a meadow filled with white daisies and secured by heavy pines. A small guest house sat alongside the daisy field.

Of all the places I have lived in my life, my summers on Islesboro are the most sacred. Our property was a true hermitage separate from, but near to, so many good friends. Their friendships still remain and always will. As Divine Providence eventually brought me, after Georgetown and some years on Wall Street, to a life of university teaching, I was privileged to enjoy nearly twenty adult summers without interruption on Islesboro while preparing my classes for the following academic year. Family and friends would come each summer for a visit. Sadly, my father had died at the age of sixty-three before the purchase of either the Damariscotta or Islesboro house. He would have loved both. He, mother, and I loved the sea.

Mother's last summer on Islesboro was when she was eighty-four. That year, as she and I walked down the Yacht Club pier to join friends on their boat for a long day's sail, she hesitated in a way I had not witnessed ever before. She had never refused sailing, from the days of Boothbay Harbor's sails out to Squirrel Island when she would tie me to the mast with a long cord to keep me in the boat, until now in her eighties. I asked her midway down the pier, having descended the ramp from the upper pier, if she were all right. She replied, "Yes, I'm fine, but I think I'll not sail today," and with her typical discretion—especially if referring to herself—said, "The pier this year seems a bit shaky. I would prefer to return to the Yacht Club porch. Catherine will come down and we will spend the day on the porch." Aunt Catherine was visiting from Washington. She hated sailing and loved gardening. The yard always improved when she came.

Returning from sailing in the late afternoon, my hosts handed me binoculars to locate the mooring. I spied my mother and Catherine still on the Club porch. They had spent the entire day together eating and visiting and were smiling. Mother never again went sailing nor walked on the Yacht Club pier.

I thank God for all those years. I learned that life is indeed a blessing and also, at times, very tragic. I learned that the principal gift of my father's family was their love of life and business. They also accepted the challenge, and possessed the drive, to succeed. The tragedies in my father's family came, I believe, from a lack of friendship with each other. It has extended even into the two generations that follow mine. One of my Tracy cousins recently said at my brother's funeral, "George, we have no family any more. We are all so diversified and so divided—and yet there is so much wealth." We agreed that we, as a family, had a serious problem. So much emphasis on the world—generation after generation—and so few seemed to be happy.

I have seen a systematic spiritual bankruptcy make its way into the clan. The tragedies of divorces and suicides have, in fact, not been absent from either side of my family. One can suffer much amidst the plenty. I have always held my suffering in the privacy of my hermit's heart, known to a few of my friends, but rarely shared within our family circle. The details need not be told here. My suffering has given me a very clear understanding of a deep disease in the lives of many families whom I have known—the disease of the "Poverty of Affluence" manifest by spiritual bankruptcy. Recognition of the "Poverty of Affluence" will be a key to understanding the solutions offered in Part II of this book.

The major turning point for me, a totally new understanding of life's purpose, came as a blessing from heaven. I went to Calcutta to be with Mother Teresa and her Sisters of the Missionaries of Charity in 1978 as a lay volunteer. There among the poor of the streets I was reborn with a rebirth that eventually led to my present mission of addressing the poverty of affluence.

Mother Teresa's presence was used by God to bring me through grace, in all my affluent poverty, to accept the beautiful poverty of the Roman Catholic priesthood, and to surrender to Christ. At the time of my ordination, Mother Teresa gave me one of her greatest gifts. She asked me never to accept any major inheritance of money from my family because I must begin with nothing in life as a priest except Jesus. It was the advice of wisdom to which I agreed.

In closing this phase of my autobiographical reminiscences I want to acknowledge that it was through my mother's family that my interest in virtue, in diplomacy, and in serving the economically poor was born. Sensitivity to her side of my family had much to do with leading me into advanced education, into extensive travel abroad, and into the heart of Calcutta. My mother, for much of her adult life, served on the Board of Directors of the House of the Good Shepherd in Hartford, which assured proper care for young ladies assigned there by the courts or received because of pregnancy outside of marriage. Many gifts in that part of my family stemmed, I believe, from their beautiful Quaker heritage.

When I was ordained to the priesthood I thanked from the altar my Catholic relatives for their gift of the Roman Catholic Church. Then I thanked my Protestant relatives, mentioning by name Uncle Taylor Gannett, whom I truly loved, for their gift of Christianity. I thanked Mother Teresa and her Sisters, who filled seven rows in the Church, for sharing with me their undivided love for Christ seen in the poor of the streets. Mother missed the actual ceremony, as her plane was late arriving from Tokyo, but joined us when I celebrated Mass later at her Washington Convent.

I believe I may have been a difficult person to know, in many ways, with my inherited mixture of pride, set against a periodic momentary lack of confidence. When this appeared in public it would confuse people. For the most part this has passed. I am now told, in my adult years, that I remain difficult to know because of an openness of heart overlain by an extreme desire for privacy—a mixture which also seems to be an occasional cause of confusion in my ordained life.

I was taught in my early years by my father that "a gentleman **never** asks anyone a personal question when a new friendship is formed. People should be allowed to tell about themselves only what they want others to know." This implied that there is a proper sense of privacy. Thus my child's heart grew protected by an intense sense of privacy which is still at the core of my being. Yet I cannot close my heart to love, or close my mind from embracing all that I see or understand as good or bad. Such a disposition can birth great joy, a joy that stems from giving meaning, in terms of Christ, to the endless realities of evil in the world. Mother Teresa, my mentor for fourteen years, taught me that the world that accepts grace and the world that seems to refuse grace are juxtaposed. She taught me that not only was I called to accept grace, but that I was being called to live a life of intense sacrificial love, both in the giving of love, and in receiving love. Thus I would come to know the true joy of the cross which is at the center of a Eucharistic life.

For me one of the greatest tragedies of the human race is that so many of us choose to assess others with negative evaluations. Perhaps that is done to preclude friendships with defective persons who, nevertheless, may have been placed in our path by Christ to be loved. I often wonder if the practice of assessing others negatively contributes to what John Paul II calls "the culture of death." Do we really live Christ's command, "Love one another as I have loved you"?

One of the greatest gifts for all persons is the acceptance with love of God's desire to bestow on us His presence by humbling us until nothing else remains. My principal model for learning how to understand life as a joyful process of knowing Our Lord while enduring humiliations came from my mother. I now realize that she was a caretaker of souls.

At the outbreak of World War II she, like so many others, went every evening to church to pray the Stations of the Cross. I was six that year and as church was so near to our home in Connecticut, she often allowed me to come with her. I was somewhat intimidated by the Stations of the Cross. They were placed on the walls of our Gothic church in dark corridors of pillars. I was not sure I wanted to spend much time in those areas. Thus I developed my own prayer routine, well in charge of my early self-determination. I would begin with my mother at the gold gates of the central altar rail. We would kneel together and I would say my own prayer to Our Lord, "I adore you, O Lord, and I praise you, President of the Blessed Sacrament." Mother never corrected my prayer, and it remained that way until I learned that Jesus was "present" and not "President." I was not too concerned about the difference. Then mother would begin her mission, with various friends, to pray for an end to the war.

I went next to Our Lady at her altar to ask her to make me a good boy, and off I went to sit in a pew in the front right corner of the church. The stained glass windows, made in France, were large and of beautiful colors. The particular window that attracted me, illumined every night by a large spotlight on the back of the rectory, depicts the angel Gabriel handing Jesus a chalice in the Garden of Gethsemane. I could not fail to sit in front of that window. I seemed to be riveted to it, and I still am whenever I return to that place. I would talk to Jesus and the angel until the ladies saying the stations would begin to come up this darkened side aisle. I could hear them getting nearer. Then I would tell Jesus that I did not know what the angel was giving to Him, but if He needed to receive it, then someday I wanted it too.

In 1984 at my ordination to the Sacred Priesthood of Melchizedek I received my chalice. Every day of my life I ask my Lord's forgiveness for giving Him such a battle in getting me to that ordination. Both of my families taught me, each in its own way, to love the grand life. I loved it too long. The gift of ordination has given me the long-awaited happiness and peace I never knew a human being could have.

Upon completing my prayer before that window, I would then sit on the floor in front of the statue of St. Thérèse, the Little Flower. I would light a candle and we would talk. I would smile at her and, in my mind's eye, she would smile at me. Someone had told me that she went to God by a "little way." I liked little things. I asked her every night to take me to Jesus in her little way. We would exchange roses— imaginary though they might have been. I would give her one, and she would hand me one.

Then I would go home with Mother and her friends, tagging behind while thinking of St. Thérèse. She has given me the "little way to Jesus." I pray in my heart with her daily that I will always have enough suffering to be a little priest—wherever I am asked to be. The priesthood is a life of love—a love that is sacrificial and that loves other persons and God, Father, Son, and Spirit.

Thus, my "war days" were days of great grace, unrealized by me at that time. I was given all that I asked for as a child: the chalice and a life of love on the cross. What greater gift can a person be given! I now hold the chalice filled with the Blood of Christ, and my own heart bleeds in a great anointing, as our hearts join in love. Ask and you shall receive.

## II. LIVING IN THE GIFT OF FREEDOM

Through this labyrinth of experiences a man was born from a youth. We all go through our own processes of development. My father died in 1958 following my graduation from Georgetown. He was only sixty-three. The loss of a father is a critical time for a young man. Again God's grace was present, and during the ensuing years, Uncle Taylor continued his advice to me to serve the world as a world citizen.

Two other men whom I loved also as surrogate fathers were important in guiding me through my twenties, Gerard McAllister and Admiral Hewlett Thibaud, U.S.N. In my heart I regarded them as Uncle Gerry and Uncle Bud. Each one knew my affection for them, and they knew I embraced their love for me. I acknowledge that without them I would never had made it through that decade of my life. Gerard McAllister was one of the McAllister Brothers who owned a tugboat company in New York, as did another family of Tracys.

I knew many of the children of shipping families in those years, Morans and Busheys, Moores, McCormacks, Harris—and loved the waterfront life of the city. Gerry was of great assistance to me during my first "real job" after university. I joined the Marine Midland Grace Trust Company at 120 Broadway, one block from Wall Street. After completing the training program, I was assigned to the International Banking Department. I loved being there. Life for me in New York was very natural as I had been in and out of the city since I was a very small child. My early experiences included surviving the mass transit systems daily for several years and singing with the Blue Hill Troop, Ltd., a Gilbert & Sullivan Company which raised money for charity. Music was still a cornerstone of my life along with my Church. St. Ignatius Church at East 84th Street and Park Avenue was a second home where I attended Mass almost daily and served on the parish council. Through the years at Marine Midland and through later employment working with Maurice Dare, Administrative Vice President of Squibb International, my sights were set worldwide.

I was scheduled to go to the Hong Kong office for Squibb, and I seemed to be caught in a web that involved marriage to a beautiful girl I had known since she came East to boarding school at the Connecticut Noroton Convent of the Sacred Heart. The web also included in its weaving the possibility of a vocation to the priesthood. After many discussions with a priest friend at St. Ignatius, I applied in 1962 for admission to the Society of Jesus. This particular avenue proved to be the wrong way for me to enter the ranks of the priesthood. I exercised the familiar strong will and left. Though the Jesuit novitiate was not God's complete plan for me, nonetheless, it was a very significant part of His plan. The novitiate engendered in me a desire for the contemplative life of prayer. It also gave rise to a burning desire to understand, "what is religion?"

Rather than returning to Wall Street, I undertook graduate studies at Boston College, a major Jesuit academic institution. During the course of approximately six years, building upon my A.B. in Political Science from Georgetown, I completed a course of studies culminating in an M.A. in Existential Philosophy, a Ph.L. (a Licentiate degree awarded by pontifical faculties) in Thomistic Philosophy, and a Ph.D. in the Philosophy of Religion. My principal courses centered on a study of the work of Reverend Bernard Lonergan and the writings of Father Karl Rahner on Word, Symbol, and Eucharist. During those years Boston College appointed me as a Teaching Fellow and Instructor in the Philosophy Department.

I became buried in a work that became truly a work of great love. To be so involved with academia at this level after having hated the first twelve years of school was nothing short of a miracle. Ask and you will receive. It was not until I had taught courses for many years in Father Lonergan's understanding of the patterns of human consciousness that I discovered what I can refer to as the advent of another freedom. One day while teaching at the Jesuits' Rockhurst College in Kansas City, Missouri, where I was a member of the Theology Department having moved up the professional ranks for nearly seven years, I understood in a deeper way Father Lonergan's insight spelled out in his vast text carrying the title, *Insight*. No greater gift of freedom could have been given at that time. Since that moment his methodology for knowing, and for knowing what we know as true and verifiable, has become for me the principal framework in which to carry out the life of the intellect. This method, allied to my former studies in St. Thomas, applies to all that exists.

During my graduate studies at Boston College, Father Joseph Flanagan, S.J., who was then Chairman of the Department of Philosophy and who had become an intimate friend, took me under his wing. He recognized early on what I also knew: the academic conflict between my ability to learn and the residual blocks to learning, compounded by fear. Two things he said were critical and developmental. Once, early in my relation with him, he assured me he was going to smash all my frozen concepts until I would be intellectually naked in order that I might grow in advanced studies. I got an instant stomachache. He did accomplish his task and his student grew in ways never imagined. Dyslexia and fear were conquered again.

Father Joe, I thank you. I came to understand his pedagogical method as being modeled on the paschal mystery— one must lose one's life to gain it! A year or so later he assured me that I would not really understand the universal application of Father Lonergan's methodology until I had taught it to other students, maybe for years. It was five years after that statement that the insight came. It embraced every dimension of my personal and professional life. It took another three or four years with the assistance of Father Robert Costello, S.J., Professor in the Psychology Department at Rockhurst and later Provincial of the Missouri Province, for me to enter into a deeper self-possession. I did not become a Jesuit priest, but I give all honor to the Society of Jesus for the deepening of my life—from Georgetown onward. Thank you, St. Ignatius, for following God's call to found the Jesuits with St. Francis Xavier and Peter Faber.

The Kansas City years provided the joy of new friendships within the Church. Father Joseph Flanagan's brother, Father James Flanagan, a priest of the Diocese of Boston was living in Kansas City in the Society of Our Lady of the Most Holy Trinity—a community of laity, priests and sisters. Father Jim answered a call to begin this community in the 1950s, and it was now living under the protection of the late Roman Catholic Bishop of Kansas City, His Excellency Bishop Cnarles H. Helmsing. When I arrived to teach at Rockhurst College I became associated with the Society as a friend and the Society invited me to live with them.

Through Fr. Jim I came to know Bishop Helmsing and the Rt. Reverend Arthur Vogel, the Episcopal Bishop of Western Missouri. Bishop Vogel was then the American appointee to the ongoing ten year A.R.C.I.C. (Anglican-Roman Catholic International Conference) organized by the Church of England and the Vatican. Discussions searching for ways to reunite these two major Churches succeeded in producing magnificent documents showing mutual agreement in areas of theology making a reunion possible. Sadly, that magnanimous and scholarly ten-year work devoted to our unity was blocked by the illegal ordination in Philadelphia of eleven women to the Episcopal priesthood by a group of retired Episcopal bishops. After four hundred years of separation, the reunion we all pray for was blocked.

During these Kansas City years I maintained an association with Bishop Vogel through his invitation to develop a program for the education of deacons for his Diocese. Bishop Helmsing approved, and Rockhurst offered the use of their classrooms. This program lasted for several years, and culminated in an invitation from Dr. Norman Pittenger of Kings College, Cambridge, a leading theologian of the Anglican Church, to become a Visiting Scholar at Cambridge as a member of St. Edmund's College. This position also carried with it a life membership in St. Edmund's and introduced a period of more freedom that broadened my horizons to the needs of a wider world. I have maintained my membership at St. Edmund's and visit the College often. Father Frank McHugh, former Dean of St. Edmund's, a friend and colleague, is now the director of the Von Hugel Institute of Ethics at St. Edmund's.

The year 1978–1979 brought with it not only the invitation to become a Visiting Scholar at Cambridge but the opportunity to accept an invitation given by Mother Teresa in 1976 at the Eucharistic Congress in Philadelphia to come to Calcutta "to let the poor teach you many things you need to know." Mother Teresa spoke about women to thousands at that Congress, which was held in a football stadium.

Through the generosity of Bishop Vogel, who was the principal speaker on the Eucharist in Protestant worship, I was asked to give a small paper as a respondent. En route to the Bellevue Stratford Hotel Ballroom where Bishop Vogel was to speak along with various respondents, I asked an usher for directions to an empty room where I might rehearse my response. He directed me to a room nearby. When I pushed open the door, I heard a loud thud followed by a groan. Nervously peeking inside, I saw a white and blue blob collapsed on the floor. It was Mother Teresa! I had knocked her over. I rushed to her aid and apologized profusely, only to hear her say: "I'm looking for the Catholic respondent to the Episcopal talk on the Eucharist. George Tracy is his name. You wouldn't be he would you?" In disbelief I responded: "Yes I am."

That shocking moment led to a half hour visit which she, in her great charity, requested, while insisting that she was not hurt. Little did we know that a lifelong friendship would result through which this young professor would experience many conversions and increases of freedom brought about by the Missionaries of Charity and their endless prayers before God.

While at Cambridge I received an invitation from Abbot Michael Abdo, O.C.S.O. of the Trappist monastery in Snowmass, Colorado to attend a meeting at the Benedictine ashram of Father Bede Griffiths in Tamil-Nadu, India, south of Madras. A group of people would be present to study manuscripts of Father Merton, who had died in Bangkok. I knew the Trappists well. My first visit to their monasteries was at Berryville, Virginia in 1954 when I was at Georgetown. Forty-two years later I visit regularly their monastery of St. Joseph in Spencer, Massachusetts to pray and to receive spiritual direction from a holy priest. Father Raphael Simon, who wrote the preface for this book, is likewise a member of that community. Along with Maine and the Jesuits, the Trappists have been key constants in my life. I accepted the invitation to go to south India.

Mother Teresa and I had many visits between 1976 and 1978 during her visits to the United States. She would write a note to meet her here and there. Each time she would delve deeply into my life, moving me to thoughts of the priesthood. I resisted. She would insist that I come to India, for she saw it was needed for my surrender to God's will. I resisted. Finally she said that Satan had me by the back of my neck. That got my attention. With tears welling up, I responded loudly, "How?"

This conversation took place in a small corner of a pantry shaped room behind a white curtain at her convent during one of her visits to New York at East 145th Street and Third Avenue. I saw my life's experiences flash past me. At this moment I was a theology and philosophy professor involved in the Church and once again considering marriage to another beautiful girl, who was trained by the Religious of the Sacred Heart and who even had her M.A. in Theology.

I asked, "What are you saying, Mother?" She replied: "When Satan cannot succeed in getting a soul in his usual way he comes after it as an 'Angel of Light'—as Lucifer. He fills your mind and heart with many good things. Look at yourself with me now. Listen to what I say. You have developed many talents. You are involved in many good things—with students, in the Church, on Boards of Directors, and with the possibility of marriage again." She listed so many things.

Then she continued, "Nothing you are doing is itself bad. In the eyes of the world it is quite beautiful to see someone so busy. Remember Satan has no body. He is a spirit. If he cannot get your soul through the life of the body, which he does not really understand, he goes after the spirit where he is a master. He has kept you very busy doing many good things in order to keep you away from the one thing God wants you to do. You must slow down and come to see India and work and pray with us before you do anything else." She then went on to explain why the West, and the United States in particular, are the poorest places in the world.

I will never forget that conversation. I knew God was speaking to me through her, and wondered how I would be able to get time to go to India. The answer was before me now. The invitation to go to Cambridge was followed within a few weeks by the invitation to come to Father Bede's monastery in Tamil-Nadu. I knew I was losing control of events. At the same time I felt myself grounded by a peace that I had longed for but had never known. By intuition, I knew humans were meant to have that kind of peace. Through these moments of new freedom, from the dyslexia insight at Dartmouth to this strange conversation between Mother and George, sitting on two little white stools closed into a space the size of a closet, I realized that the reconstruction of a human being was taking place. I departed from her convent in peace and wonder.

I left Madras, my first stop in India, with two profound remembrances. One morning while I was walking in a tiny village in conversation with a colleague from Cambridge, I stopped to talk with a young boy who was reading an English New Testament. He greeted us with a huge smile. I asked him if he were Christian. He replied, "Oh no, I am not a Christian, but I like your Jesus very much! I cannot be a Christian." We asked him to explain why he could not be a Christian, although he loved Jesus very much. He explained that he "could not be a Christian because he would have to kill people. You know," he said, "all the Christian nations go to war and kill each other. If I am a Christian I would have to go to war and kill people. I am a boy of peace and must stay Hindu. But I do like your Jesus very much."

This was one of the many profound lessons I learned in India. Hopefully that beautiful young man is still reading his New Testament. I pray for him very often. Another morning while bathing about 5:00 AM in a small river near the monastery, I watched the sun rise through stripes of yellow, purple, and dark orange framing pointed mountains that looked as though they were specially carved by God just for the Orient. I was alone in a place I did not know, with strangers (with the exception of a very few people) at this conference, and traveling with only a small pack that could be carried on my shoulders. Yet never could I have anticipated the happiness and peace of my soul.

With the conference over, Calcutta was next. Calcutta cannot be described. I spent the first night sitting in a window seat watching people sleep in the street and wander through it. Not everyone who slept got up. A bull cart passed through in the morning and picked up a few who had died. I slept through the morning and went to the Missionaries of Charity in the afternoon. I rang the bell. A sister answered the door. I introduced myself by name to the very small, smiling nun, and to my astonishment her eyes opened wide and she said, "Oh, come in and go up to the chapel. I will get Mother. You know we are expecting you." I asked her how that could be possible as no notice had been sent ahead. She smiled again and said, "Oh, you are one of the people we pray for by name every day. Mother says they will all come when it is time. I will get her. She will be glad to see you." The stomach-ache was coming again! Mother arrived in the chapel for our visit.

The first person in India who asked me for help was a very old thin man. He was clothed in a minimal white cloth around his waist and another around his head. He was missing one arm to the elbow and one leg to the knee. He was dirty and had bugs. He stretched out his one arm and the other half-arm. Staring into my soul he said quietly, "Help me." I froze. In that instant I was overcome with a mixture of emotions that swirled inside my head. I was confused, and I ran away like someone on fire, I reached the chapel, fell prostrate, and wept like a child. I had come in touch with my "poverty of affluence" and knew why Mother was insisting that I come to India. It was impossible to give my brother—a son of God—what he needed. The days passed in Calcutta with challenges too many to mention. Often Mother had long visits with me.

During another visit, Mother was equally as direct. "George, one day you will be a priest. It's what Jesus wants. Where would you like to be a priest?" I replied that I had three choices; Connecticut, New York City, or Maine. I was not sure. She told me to pray over it. A few days later I said: "Should I decide to become a priest, I would rather grow old in the countryside of Maine than in Manhattan." After I had heard the call in 1982 she gave me a letter addressed to Bishop O'Leary of Portland, Maine to present to him.

When she asked how I liked Calcutta, I reminded her about my refusal to help the old man. She nodded and asked me to continue. Then I shared with her the fact that I felt as though I had at last found the face of Christ. "How is that?" she asked. I said, "Mother I have never seen so much poverty and at the same time such joy on people's faces. It is the crucifixion and resurrection all at once." Mother took my hands and, her eyes dancing with joy, responded with her now very familiar statement: "Acha . . . you have found Jesus. You know now why we are here. It is the face of Christ all day." I did not want to leave.

Her last instruction was to spend every Saturday morning, when I went back to North America, in prayer before the Eucharist, from nine until noon, in her contemplative convent at 160th Street and Union Avenue in New York. The sisters would give me lunch and, if I wished, I could work with them in the afternoon. "But," I objected, "won't I be in the sisters' way?" And "What if they are not expecting me?" She stopped me cold with the look that all who have lived with her know. It is a look that goes to the soul and silences every possible sound, and one knows that what she says is coming from God. That put an end to my apology. She said, "George, you will go there and pray. I have already phoned Sister Nirmala, the superior, and the sisters are expecting you."

I returned to Cambridge via Rome where I visited Brother Sebastian, the head of Mother's newly formed institute for contemplative priests. On the underground from Heathrow to Liverpool station to connect with the train to Cambridge, something happened. I had made this trip many times. But this day it was wholly new. I realized again why I had gone to Calcutta. The train into London was passing station after station at the beginning of rush hour. My eyes were frozen, gazing at my fellow passengers: 1. We all had clothes on 2. All had shoes on 3. We all had some money in our pockets or we would not have been riding on this train 4. Many had bags of groceries on their laps for the evening meal 5. Many had hats on 6. Many were reading—they *could* read 7. NO ONE WAS SMILING! Every Indian—so often with nothing—smiles!

Here it was, Mother's definition of the West staring me in the face. We are the poorest countries in the world because we are spiritually bankrupt.

During this last visit prior to my departure, Mother reviewed various tenets of the Missionaries of Charity—those areas of service to the poor she hoped would be accomplished as the years passed. They are listed by number and often found framed or painted on the walls of the convent parlors. One of these is that they would take the undivided love of Jesus to those who suffer from the loss of Christ, where His presence has been disguised by the world of materialism. With that having been said, she again looked through me with that look that goes to the soul and said, "George, you will be a priest. And you will one day, as a priest, bring this undivided love of Christ to those who are suffering from the poverty of affluence. Jesus wants you to do that because you were born into it and you will understand their problems when you go to them as a priest. Some will listen and many will not. When I bring my cup of water and loaf of bread to the poor to whom Jesus sends me, they smile and take it because they know they are hungry. When you and those who live and work with you bring your cup of water and loaf of bread to your poor, the doors will often slam in your face because they do not know they are so poor and so hungry for God. My job is much easier than yours will be, but Jesus and his Mother will bring those to your work who will be able to do the job. You must become a community of undivided love."

My whole being was silenced and my heart was melting in joy. The stomach-ache had disappeared, yet in a small place somewhere inside I could feel the old resistance waiting to raise its familiar head. This day there was no fear, and I left for Rome allowing God's mercy and love to show me life as I had never seen it before. When I returned to the United States it seemed more evident than ever that we do not know how to die to self in order to rise.

I prayed in New York every Saturday morning from 9 to 12 from September 1979 through the end of February 1980, except for Christmas week. I was now teaching at St. John's University, doing volunteer work at Covenant House, and living with the Brothers of the French Taize community, who had a residence in New York. This proved to be a fruitful period. The sisters at the contemplative convent were wonderfully kind and generous. They welcomed me weekly for three hours of private prayer before the Eucharist in their chapel.

One Saturday in February I was sitting on the chapel floor. There

were no chairs. The floor was cold. There was no heat. Ice was forming on the windows. It was a very bitter New York winter day. Clothed
in blue jeans, ski socks, a sweater, a ski jacket, and asking Our Lord's
permission, I covered my head with a wool ski hat. I engaged in a
heart to heart conversation with our Lord, reminding Him that I still
wanted to be married and have ten children. He knew there had been
three splendid opportunities; two married others and the third died
suddenly while in law school. I never let go of this desire to marry. In
frustration I blurted out, "Jesus, I don't want to be celibate. I want to
be married and have ten children." In a way I have come to understand Jesus in prayer I heard Him say: "You don't have to be celibate
to be a priest."

A deep internal quiet came over me and, in my own way of understanding Jesus in prayer, I heard Him say: "You don't have to be
celibate to be a priest." Shocked, I asked, "What did You say?"

> You don't have to be celibate to be a priest. George, when it
> comes to Me you have everything inside out. I want you in
> the priesthood. All you have to do is get small enough, even
> for one minute, and let Me in. Just let Me in and I will be
> Priest in you. It's not your priesthood, it's Mine! It's not your
> celibacy, it's Mine! I will be celibate in you. It is not your chas-
> tity, it's Mine! I will be chaste in you. It is not your poverty, its
> Mine! I will be poor in you. You have nothing to worry about.
> All you have to do is to show up every day and I, as Priest in
> you, will take you wherever I want you to go in the world. Just
> let me in.

My mind went into racing mode just as it had in India the day I
refused to help the old man with one arm and one leg. And once
again I fell prostrate on the cold chapel floor and cried like a child for
a very long time and said, "Yes, Lord—may your Father's will be done.
I will come to you in your priesthood. Please never leave me. I will
never make it without you."

Having pulled myself together in prayer, I left the chapel for lunch.

Sister Nirmala passed me in the hall. She must have seen red eyes. Today must be the day, she said in her quiet way. "Call Mother!" I had finally let go and let God in.

When after some time I had finally set my affairs in order, Mother gave me a letter dated June 8, 1982:

8/6/82

Dear Bishop O'Leary,

   I would be very grateful if you bless and allow George Tracy to be the Priest of Jesus through your hands.

   My gratitude is my prayer for you.

God bless you.

M. Teresa MC

Copy of the Autograph of Mother Teresa's Letter to Bishop O'Leary

I called the Bishop asking to visit him at his home. It was the spring vacation at St. John's and the time to go to Maine to open our house for the summer, and the time to tell the Bishop my story.

Bishop O'Leary accepted me for the Diocese of Portland after the application process was completed. He was puzzled about how to arrange my studies for the priesthood as I had already taught nearly all the courses necessary for ordination except Canon Law. He consulted with Cardinal Baum's office in Rome, where educational decisions are made. It was decided that I could reside for two years at the North American College in Rome, at Catholic University in Washington, or at the Catholic Theological Union in Chicago. I was not to take any courses other than Canon Law. Rather, I was to find three pastoral jobs for two years and place myself under approved spiritual direction. The two years would be under the overall supervision of the major seminary rector at whichever university was decided upon. I chose Catholic University in Washington. My mother was aging and trips could easily be made to Connecticut to see her.

Rome's wishes were fulfilled. For the two years prior to ordination, I worked under the tutelage of Monsignor John Murphy, the Pastor, who had also been Rector of the National Shrine of the Immaculate Conception on the campus of the Catholic University of America. Ordination to the priesthood took place on the feast of the Immaculate Heart of Mary, June 30, 1984 at St. Joseph's Church on Capitol Hill in Washington, D.C.

Bishop O'Leary had ordained me as deacon in Camden, Maine in the preceding March. The church had been full. Other than those on the altar, only six Catholics were present. Bishop O'Leary gave a beautiful talk on ecumenism to the congregation of two hundred and fifty.

The ordination to the priesthood was a blessed event. Bishop O'Leary had asked the permission of the Washington Archdiocese for my ordination to take place in the Archdiocese where I had trained. My mother would be able to share her joy with her Gannett cousins whom we loved. It would also be easier for her to travel to Washington rather than to the coast of Maine. The ordaining bishop was the late Bishop Amadee Proulx, Auxiliary of the Diocese of Portland.

The church was filled with friends from many years and many places. I am sure each of them had nine reasons why I should not be doing this. I was reminded that day by two priests dear to my heart, by the first that Jesus picks the poorest of the poor to be his priests, and if he had to look all over the United States He could not find a greater mess than I. Therefore I qualified. The second, Father Joseph Babendrier of Opus Dei, whom I love as a brother, hurried up to me in the sacristy and put his arm around my shoulder and said, "From this day forward you have one important thing to do—and that is to say Mass every day. Everything else is baloney!"

I was allowed by the Diocese of Portland to retain my association with Father James Flanagan while remaining incardinated in the Diocese. At this time in the development of Father's Society, priests were loaned to work with him, as is true with other religious societies. When after many years of growth, Father Flanagan's Society received Rome's approval, the priests who were working with Father Flanagan had to decide whether they would remain incardinated in their own diocese or become incardinated in his Society. I chose to remain incardinated in the diocese with the consent of our new Bishop, Joseph Gerry, O.S.B., a former Benedictine Abbot of St. Anselm's Abbey in New Hampshire.

After my ordination, I served with the U.S. Navy as a Chaplain to the U.S. Marine Corps for eleven years, on active duty in Asia and California and then reserve duty in Washington, South Carolina, and Virginia. In 1995 I returned to my diocese to become Pastor of St. Mary's Church in Orono, Maine, home of the University of Maine.

So be it! This autobiographical sketch has been accomplished in accordance with the request of my mentors at St. Joseph's Trappist Monastery in Spencer, Massachusetts. The "who" and the "where" surrounding the events are secondary to the principal message of conversion which never ends.

For years upon years God tried to slow me down to hear His call. I do believe Mother Teresa's statement that there is really one vocation for all persons: living an undivided love for Jesus Christ. Once we begin to do that, He then shows us how He wants us to carry that out. Within the undivided love for Himself that He put into my heart, which grew through so many years and experiences, He was also calling me to the priesthood. That was His wish.

Often I am told that I had a "late vocation"—being ordained to the priesthood at forty-nine years of age. To say that, I believe, is to misunderstand vocation. Our vocation is continuous according to Scripture, where we are told that "from your mother's womb you have been called." I have discovered that one's vocation unfolds in stages.

Therein lies the point of this story—the examination in depth of the reader's own life of vocation, in order to discover what form it might take. From our mothers' wombs we have been called. To become a person, as our Creator wishes, is an ongoing process with years of preparation and years of service to His Kingdom. The call, like ourselves, is eternal—yet has a before, a present, and an after. A truly successful human life can only be attributed to one who has fulfilled God's will.

Mary, the Mother of Our God and our human model, gave us the most important words we can ever say during our passage on earth, "Be it done unto me according to your word." Nothing else is more important. When priests can speak these words from their hearts and pronounce on earth the words of the consecration of the Mass, their humanity fulfills Scripture, unites heaven and earth, and they live not only as cooperators but also as co-redeemers with God, completing on earth what was not completed in Jesus. They can then teach the laity to live as co-redeemers.

When I read the *Seven Storey Mountain* at seventeen, Thomas Merton prepared me for the journey that followed. He wrote, "You shall taste the solitude of My anguish and My poverty, and I shall lead you into the high places of My joy, and you shalll die in Me and find all things in My mercy, which has created you for this end and brought you from Prades to Bermuda to St. Antonin, to Oakham, to London, to Cambridge, to Rome, to New York, to Columbia, to Corpus Christi, to St. Bonaventure, to the Cistercian Abbey of the poor men who labor in Gethsemani, that you may become the brother of

God, and learn to know the Christ of the burnt men."

Today I know my Lord as Lord, who teaches me in prayer. He comes to me and forms me in His own Gethsemane and in His Resurrection. He takes pieces of my body away and he takes pieces of my mind away, according to Our Father's will. As I watch them disappear little by little, day by day, I rejoice with increasing joy, my heart nearly bursting with love as I utter,

TAKE THIS ALL OF YOU, AND EAT IT: THIS IS MY BODY WHICH WILL BE GIVEN UP FOR YOU, and

TAKE THIS ALL OF YOU, AND DRINK FROM IT: THIS IS THE CUP OF MY BLOOD. THE BLOOD OF THE NEW AND EVERLASTING COVENANT. IT WILL BE SHED FOR YOU AND FOR ALL SO THAT SINS MAY BE FORGIVEN. DO THIS IN MEMORY OF ME.

I have been called from all eternity from my mother's womb from Hartford Hospital, where I came into this life, to Bristol, to New York, to Boothbay Harbor in Maine, to Islesboro, to Washington, to London, to Kansas City, to Montreal, to Cambridge, to Fatima, to Madras, to Fr. Bede's Shantivanam monastery, to Calcutta, to Manila, to Buenos Aires, to San José in Costa Rica, and, most importantly, to the Trappist Monasteries of Snowmass in Colorado, Berryville in Virginia, Spencer in Massachusetts, Guimaras in the Philippines, and to the Benedictines of Weston, Vermont and Abiquiu, New Mexico, to the Diocese of Portland, Maine, and to the priesthood of Jesus Christ. I have learned that Christ loves us while He allows us to be burned and humbled as we share in His crucifixion. I have been allowed to embrace the meaning of life knowing that THE EUCHARIST IS THE CENTER OF LIFE—where all that is exists.

## A BRIDGE TO THE DIALOGUES

A few statements are necessary to bridge Part I with Part II which exposes my life of prayer. My overall intention has been stated: to learn to listen to our experiences and to our God. A detailed record of my life as a priest is not necessary for this book. To provide it would be to betray the intention of this sharing. I do find it necessary, however, to refer to a few events in my life since ordination which are essential to the beginning of the Cor Christi Trinitatis Institute.

My first assignment as a priest was to the United States Navy as a chaplain, originally offered to me by Admiral James Watkins U.S.N (Ret.) while on a boat celebrating the birthday of his son, now Father James Watkins of the Diocese of Washington, D.C. The Church approved and I went to Chaplains' Training School in Newport, Rhode Island. My principal tours of duty were with the Air Wing of the United States Marine Corps. The Navy Chaplains serve the Navy, the Marine Corps, and the Coast Guard. No words could be written in a small space to express my gratitude to Admiral Watkins, my Bishop, and my Lord for allowing me to serve his poor in this way. Friendships have been made for life in the Navy and Marine Corps. Perhaps that period of my life can be reserved for another book. Many vocations exist in the military. The men and women in the services want truth in every category. When they get it they respond with all they have to maintain a just world through sacrifice founded on sacrificial love.

I cannot pass over my tour in the Philippines without mentioning the impact of that time on my military and spiritual formation. The significant people who were used by Providence for that purpose were first of all my Commanding Officer, Colonel William Sweeney, U.S.M.C., and his wife Ann. They were the parents of ten children, three of their own and seven adopted from various parts of the world. All seven were handicapped in some way. While we were at Subic Bay they were honored by President Reagan as the military family of the year. Secondly, my spiritual formation was influenced by the people of the Philippines. They, like the people of India, are God's children. I believe they will one day move through China and middle Europe and then to the West as they carry out what may be their destiny to reevangelize the world. I was recently in Manila during the Holy Father's visit when nearly five million people gathered in Luneta Park to attend his Mass. At his last homily he, too, spoke of their call to evangelize the world.

Early in my tour in the Philippines I was privileged to have a visit with His Eminence Jaime Cardinal Sin, the Archbishop of Manila—another act of Providence. As the months passed by, he extended many invitations to me to come to his home for dinner and to stay overnight. During this time the country passed through the Marcos Revolution. I watched and listened in awe to this great and holy priest of the Eucharist as he instructed me in his love for the Sacred Heart of Jesus and the Immaculate Heart of Mary.

Over the months a profound friendship developed. He sacrificed much to train this new priest well. His love was immense and often corrective. I admired his ability to be a true father to a new priest even though our ages were not too far apart. More than any priest I have known, he was singled out by God to be part of my life for this purpose. I wonder sometimes if I would have made it through those years without his advice.

One day he said to me, "Father George, we need a new work in the world—a work like that which Ignatius did. Our world is similar to his. In both 1535 and 1986-7, the divinity of Christ is denied everywhere. We do not have the time to respond as Ignatius did by building schools and universities. We must do it by persuading the leaders of the world, who are tempted daily by materialism and affluence, to dedicate themselves to Christ's teaching. We must bring His love to them and, through their conversion, bring them back to seeing the Eucharist as central to their lives. Let us give retreats. Will you join me on your free days?" I quickly responded with an enthusiastic, "Yes, your Eminence. I will ask my military superiors for permission." Permission was granted.

Then and there I shared with him Mother Teresa's insights into the poverty of affluence. He knew her well and loved her very much. He said that the next time she came to Manila the three of us would talk about such a work. We met, we talked, we prayed. The work was slowly born through different and beautiful moments.

Our first retreat was to twenty-four of President Marcos' generals and admirals, all of whom were on active duty. The second was to the chaplains of the armed forces, the third to leaders in business. The seed of what is now the Cor Christi Trinitatis Institute in the United States and Cor Christi, Ltd. in the United Kingdom was planted in the Republic of the Philippines.

Support poured out from many families. To list them all would fill another book. Special thanks must be given, to the families: Afable, Mapas, Ybiernas, Araneta, Telesco, Achacosa, Davis, Sweeney, and to the Ongsiaka and Sanidad families, whose support came later.

Finally, through the Papal Nuncio to the Philippines, Archbishop Bruno Torpigliani, this potential work was brought to the attention of an Archbishop in the Vatican. It was the wish of the Papal Nuncio that a determination be made as to whether I should begin Cor Christi or apply to the Academia, the Papal School for Diplomacy. The decision was reached to begin Cor Christi. This interview in Rome was one of the most blessed days of my short priesthood. I was happy to learn that the Holy Father was placing great trust in the many new works that were coming forth in the Church for its renewal. My prayer remains, if Cor Christi is to be one of these works, may we suffer sufficiently to be a force for Christ in this contemporary world.

Father Tracy at First Holy Communion, Bristol Connecticut - above
and at First Mass, St. Joseph's Church, Capitol Hill, Washington, DC

Federal Hill Green, St. Joseph's Church in distance, seen from Tracy Home - top
Tracy Home on Bellevue Avenue, seen from Federal Hill Green - below

Window, St. Joseph's Church, from which Fr. Tracy received
childhood inspirations - above
St. Joseph's Church and Rectory on Federal Hill - below

St. Mary's Church and Rectory, Orono, Maine, a University town, home of the University of Maine

His Holiness at prayer following his private morning Mass. Fr. Tracy is present as an invited concelebrant.

His Eminence Jaime Cardinal Sin, Archbishop of Manila, and Fr. Tracy at lunch in Manila. Below: LCDR Michael Waters, USN, a Co-Founder of Cor Christi on roof terrace of Navy Offices, London, England.

Major Scott Buran, USMC, a Co-Founder of Cor Christi, and Ann, at their
wedding at Castine, Maine, August 27,1994, with Fr. Tracy

Chapel at Mother House, Missionaries of Charity in Calcutta - top
Children of Calcutta loved by Mother Teresa and her sisters - below

The Clergy in procession with Fr. Tracy in the central group at the Eucharistic Congress in Poland.

Cor Christi members from U.S.A. walking from Wroclaw Cathedral at the Eucharistic Congress.
Left to right: Kathy Wirth, Dr. Frank Agnone, Octavia Dugan, Mary Ann Becksted

Cor Christi members at Eucharistic Congress in Poland - top
Elizabeth Rylands, Lady Deirdre McNair-Wilson, and Courtenay Whedbee
being entertained in home of a young Polish couple. - below

At the Eucharistic Congress, Poland, left to right:
Tom Grobel, Regional Director for UK, Dr. Hugh McGrath, Regional Director in
New Orleans, LA, and seminarian Peter Conroy, assistant to Fr. Tracy

Dr. Ivan and Laura Garcia with Fr. Tracy at the Eucharistic Congress

Frs. Mark Elvins and Tracy, 25th generation cousins and direct descendants of the two knights who killed St. Thomas Becket in Canterbury Cathedral in 1170.

R.C. Mass of reparation in Canterbury Cathedral celebrated by Frs. Elvins, Tracy, and Harvey, with permission of the Anglican and R.C. Churches.

A monthly Cor Christi meeting for greater Baltimore-Washington DC group in Courtenay Whedbee's garden - top

A New Orleans Cor Christi group meeting at home of members "Pip" and Barbara Brennan with Francisco Stengel, member from Buenos Aires, third from left, with Fr. Tracy attending - below

Cor Christi Annual Retreat at Regency Hotel, Bar Harbor, Maine, September 1997. Members attended from USA, South America, Greece, Egypt, Central America, Puerto Rico, and the United Kingdom

Bar Harbor Retreat. United Kingdom Cor Christi members, left to right: Chantal Armstrong, Thomas Grobel, Frances Scarr, Sylvia Condylis, Lady Deirdre McNair-Wilson

Courtenay Whedbee and Vice-Admiral Jim Sagerholm, USN (Ret.), leaders of the
Baltimore-Washington group, at the Bar Harbor Retreat

Ligia Remick of Brazil and USA with Jenkins and Mary Cromwell
of Baltimore at Bar Harbor retreat

Cor Christi's youngest member: Oscar Eschandi from Egypt at Bar Harbor
Retreat

Leonides and Sylvia Condylis, members of
London group, and foundersof San José,
Costa Rica group, enjoying lobsters at a
Maine retreat

At the Orono, **Maine Retreat** of
1995: left to right:
Melinda Wayne, Jacqueline Morgan,
Fr. Tracy

Elizabeth Bibby, member of the Baltimore group, and Fr. Tracy enjoy a Cor Christi meeting.

Baroness Alexandra de Koranyi and Mary Ann Becksted at a Cor Christi Retreat. West Franklin, New Hampshire

Members Dr. Mark and Gloria Miller of Gettysburg, Pennsylvania
at West Franklin, New Hampshire annual retreat

Fr. Tracy and Alphonsus Kelly, former classmates at St. Edmund's College,
address Cor Christi members following a meeting in London

London Cor Christi members at lunch following a meeting. Left to right: Ann Hill, Lady Deirdre McNair-Wilson, and Lady Elsa Bowker

Fr. Tracy with members Ann and Dan Hill at their home in Ascot, England

Cor Christi members at a Cor Christi picnic at Boden's Ride House - home of Dan and Ann Hill in Ascot. Left to right: Franzl Forrester, Ann Hill, Tom Southern

Saint Joseph's Abbey, Spencer, Massachusetts

Fr. Tracy with Fr. Raphael Simon, O.C.S.O.

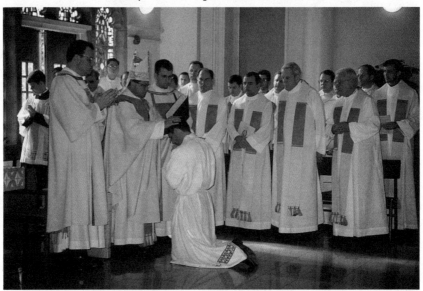

His Excellency Michael Cote, Auxiliary Bishop of Portland, Maine, ordains Peter Conroy to the Order of Deacon for the Diocese of Portland at the Catholic Univesity of America on Nov. 21, 1998. Rev. Mr. Conroy, an associate of Cor Christi, will be ordained to the priesthood June 12, 1999 at the Cathedral in Portland.

# PROLOGUE TO
## DIALOGUES IN LOVE
### FROM THE HEART OF CHRIST (COR CHRISTI )

Jesus began by reminding me of an answer He gave to me at Christ in the Desert Monastery, Abiquiu, New Mexico in November 1973. When I asked in my meditation, before sleeping in my hermitage: "Lord, who am I?" I was in great need of knowing an answer to this question at that retreat, as a powerful awareness of the spiritual life was growing. He always wants us to ask, and I asked, knowing that He would in some way answer. At 3 A.M. I awoke and went to my writing table with a desire to pray and perhaps to write. I lighted the kerosene lamp. As I sat in silence I heard in my heart very clearly, "George, you are earth, community, prayer and dance." I wrote that down in my diary. This brought me great peace. I prayed for a long time.

During the years that followed, I realized that "earth" indicated my great love for the Incarnation, and for Christ's presence in all creation. All creation is holy and sacred because it is created by God and has been invaded by God by the birth of His Son.

"Prayer" was immediately evident to me. Only in prayer are we open to God's speaking to us. Prayer provides the silence which is necessary if we are to be open to God and experience His love and learn His plan for our life in His sacred creation – earth.

"Community" was also immediately obvious—we are like our God who is a Trinity of three Persons living in a community of love, trust, and mutual care. We too, are asked to live in this way, with the Trinity as our model. We are meant to live in love with another or others. We are to live with and for others. To be of a community, no matter how modest, is fundamental to the fullness of human life which calls itself Christian. Even the widow and the hermit are in a family of love, those for whom they pray, begging God's graces upon all.

I have come to understand "dance" as a life of joy, which is always the true sign of holiness. We become joyful when we become able to give meaning to the suffering we experience, through it sharing in the crucifixion of Christ. We possess our own Good Friday, with a joy that is directly proportional to the suffering to which we give meaning in Christ. Thus I came to know who I am, earth, community, prayer and dance.

The development of my life before and after this experience at Christ in the Desert Monastery became very special. It caused me to realize that **all our lives are very special,** at the moments of greatest suffering as well as at the moments of greatest joy. The point in all that follows is that our lives are eternal; called into earthly existence from our mother's womb by name from all eternity and for all eternity. We come to earth to partake in the sacredness of creation in a community, as one united with the earth, in order to continue the process of its sanctification, by living in the model of Christ who lives in the Trinity. In this model we learn the life which enables us to return to the heart of Christ in the Trinity, when we leave the earth.

Our life is very special. Our purpose is

1. To come to earth through God's immense generosity and to love in God's love on earth for a specified period.

2. To know how to live the life of the Incarnation, respecting the sacredness of creation.

3. To cooperate with the Trinity, the Mother of God, and with each other, to build a holy world, living as co-redeemers of Jesus with Mary.

We are to live as nobility in its fullest sense for we are God's children. We are to leave this earth consumed in love with hearts which have become generous and which will be united with the heart of the Trinity, where we will know a life of generosity and love forever.

Yes, my life is very special. Yes, your life is also very special. We must never consider one person more special than any other. There are many different gifts, and many different talents. These are, for each of us, a part of His design , which is to love Him. The only gift we have, however, that qualifies us to be very special is the one gift we are all given, the gift of life.

We are to live a life of undivided love for Him, knowing that it is through the generosity of His Father's love that Jesus can know us and we can know Him. Everything else flows from that. When we enter life on earth we are positioned by Baptism to become lovers of and with Jesus. Then one day we are called out from life on earth. Our entrance and departure remain our primary framework and are the natural limits enclosing a life on earth in which we make all our choices for or against the creative love of God for us.

Why is it we devote nearly all our time on earth to so many other possibilities?

# PART II

# DIALOGUES

## 1. INSTRUCTIONS
October 20, 1991
St. Bernard's Church
Sharon, Connecticut

*I was asking Our Lord for direction in my work as a priest. He reminded me of a statement which He had made at the monastery of Christ in the Desert in Abiquiu, New Mexico: "Remember you are earth, community, prayer and dance."*

*Today I prayed for a long while before the Eucharist. The following came into my heart:.*

Never search for self, My love, search only for Me and for those whom I shall bring to you. For you will bring to Me the young for My priesthood, Father George. This is necessary for the gift of leadership I am giving you. The work of Cor Christi is for the military, the diplomatic corps, and the world of business, but it will be done through the priesthood. You cannot do it all alone, for the work is already too big and too important.

The charism at the center of the work lies in the priesthood of Melchizedek. The ordained priests are to establish in the hearts of all a burning love for the Ordained Priesthood as well as for the Royal Priesthood of the laity which is received in Baptism. It is only by grasping the reality of their priesthood that My people will understand their purpose on this earth. You must have priests ordained to do this work with you.[1] I will give you a Bishop to protect and sponsor this work who will not incur a financial or other burden in doing so. He will secure a place for you from which you can develop it.[2]

---

1. Cor Christi seminarians and priests will be incardinated in their dioceses, in which they work in accordance with the Cor Christi charism explained in these dialogues.
2. Through the gift of a benefactor Cor Christi Institute has purchased a house in Orono, Maine, where Fr. Tracy had served as Pastor. This is the central office for the work in the United States.

The format will be the same in all locations: an overlay with a seminary. Cor Christi should always be a neighbor of a seminary.

Cor Christi members will find their center in My heart, which is present in the world in the Eucharist. The formation in Eucharistic life should be central in seminaries. All members of Cor Christi will understand that their hearts overlap one another in the Eucharist, one upon the other. This will be taught by the priests of Melchizedek to the laity. The priests, one with each other and with My heart, will be united with the hearts of the laity, who will be one among themselves, as will be explained in the dialogues that follow.

This is so important because I, Jesus, the Son of God, and My love, can be known in the world only through the hearts of My own lovers. For in their hearts is life, founded upon the beautiful suffering of My heart, in whose bleeding you are washed and purified so as to come to resurrection. The bleeding that comes from suffering turns into balm and oil, anointing the body for its conversion, transfiguration, and holy resurrection.

The priesthood, Melchizedek and Royal, is the sacrificial path to resurrection. You must all know and walk this path in order to be one with Me, My Father, and the Holy Spirit. *There is no other road.* My children are not building a holy nation because they are not living a holy priesthood, ordained or lay. Never has it been more urgent to teach all people and their leaders this privilege, a privilege and an obligation, My loving Father George, My priest. I am giving you this special work for My world.

I know your pain and your own bleeding. They are necessary so that you will be able to see and experience the beautiful priesthood in the hearts of all My children. Your own suffering and bleeding must necessarily be seen by others, so that their priesthood may become known to them. Your suffering will in time become very visible. It will be that very visibility that will bring others to know their priesthood, because the visibility of your bleeding will be united with the visibility of immense joy—the kind of joy that can only come from My heart. My heart is the heart of our work.

You will in time have a Cor Christi center near a seminary in

Rome from which My heart will be taught by priests. My Mother's words will always apply: Do not ask people to join the work, offer it to them. We will bring to the work those who are meant to be part of it, who will always manifest the two signs of the charism.

Never be discouraged when a Bishop refuses the work. Move on. It is not necessary to be approved by all. Many do not even approve of Me, whom the Father wants made known fully to all His children on earth. So do not fear if the giving of My love to others through your love is often blocked. You are at that moment nearest to My own heart, and I am holding you so close to Me that we are breathing together. It is very important for you to know this. I love you so much. I never want you to be separated from Me. I wish our every breath to be drawn as one. I wish that every pain I have be yours, and that every pain you have be given back to Me, for my Father wants you to be one with Me, and I, your Lord, wish it also.

Please, My son, do not wander so far from Me. You do not pray as I wish you to pray, as we are now praying. This moment of prayer is as I wish it to be every day, never away from My breathing heart. My breathing heart bleeds in its breathing. It bleeds not only because of the sins of My children, but also because of My love for them. I breathe life into you in My agony, and in My love, which is also My joy. I bleed and breathe for you and into you, My son, when you sin, and this is what sustains you and brings you back to Me so often for forgiveness. My bleeding is a bleeding that anoints you, like a balm that bathes you, to which I often give a beautiful fragrance. This gratuitous gift is given especially to the little women who are My children.

The work of Cor Christi is to teach My heart which forms priesthood in its two levels, Melchizedek and Royal, so completely explained in this visit. You must meditate on it for long hours and unfold it. I will help you again and often. You will work all your life to establish and train the priests of Melchizedek and, through them, to develop the Royal Priesthood of the laity. I want all My children to know Me so well that we may breathe together, their heads on My chest, that they may know Me through the breathing of My bleeding heart.

Be the one to do this. Live prayer. **Be My heart.**

## 2. LISTEN
Feast of St. John the Evangelist
December 27, 1991
St. Bernard Church
Sharon, Connecticut

*In prayer before the Eucharist*
*I am sorry for not listening, Lord. I am frightened when I find myself doing that. I see a great vacuum open between us when I do not stop and listen. Please, Lord, come back. I ask forgiveness.*

No matter how briefly I speak to you in your heart, even if it is but for a moment, you must stop all you are doing, for I want to speak to your heart for that very moment. Whatever you are about to do at that moment, however insignificant it may appear, needs My presence, either directly, or through your angel who is there for Me. Come to know your angel, Father George, and you will come to know the Holy Spirit. You are given so completely to the Body of Christ, to the world, and to My Body in the Eucharist, all of which My Father desires you to touch, understand and be one with. But We are now trying to educate you to respond immediately to the Spirit, in the same way that you immediately recognize My Body in the Eucharist, in the Church, and in others who carry Me and who are called to Me in My priesthood of Melchizedek.

Amen

# 3. THE RULE 1
December 30, 1991
Feast of the Holy Family
St. Bernard Church
Sharon, Connecticut

*On this feast of the Holy Family the Lord spoke after Mass during my thanksgiving.*

Cor Christi is to have this feast day as a model.

1. Be a holy family unified in prayer.
2. Live the cross that is given to you, knowing that it is for your redemption. That is its meaning.
3. Live a joyful obedience to the Church.
4. Live with a *heart of forgiveness*, like that of Mary's heart when she held her dead Son, Me, the Lord.

My Mother's life is to be your model and rule on these four points.

Amen

## 4. HEARING

December 31, 1991
Vigil of the Feast of the Mother of God
Private Residence
Knowlton, Quebec, Canada

*Today, October 28, 1996, on the feast of Sts. Simon and Jude at St. Joseph's Abbey, Spencer, Massachusetts, I asked for help with this dialogue. Our Lord reminded me that I had lacked a quiet environment at the time this dialogue was written because a joyful and noisy dinner-dance was in progress in the main part of the home of my host. Consequently I did not accurately reproduce His words. Our Lord then supplied what was missing.*

There is an absolute unity between being preacher, priest, and listener to the Word that comes from the intrinsic unity between the Son and the Father, and Their unity with created men and women through Baptism. Authentic teaching begins with My Father. I receive it and, as Lord and High Priest, give it to My ordained priests. When they unite their teaching to My Father's teaching, and when this teaching is confirmed in prayer before the Blessed Sacrament and in the Paschal Sacrifice of the Mass, they can then teach Truth that is of the Father. *[Editor's note: Implicit in this confirmation is the correspondence of the teaching with Scripture and the Magisterium.]*

The unity among Father, Son, ordained priest, and the baptized laity is designed from eternity for the reception and reproduction of truth. This is effected through the gifts of speaking and listening. Listening is a hearing with understanding. In the priesthood of Melchizedek the priest is called to that model of hearing in which he becomes inseparable from the Father through oneness with Christ, the Son. This oneness is wholeness, which is holiness.

Cor Christi is of My heart and reveals in the eyes and hearts and lives of its members the holiness that the world must see . This holiness, recognized in lives lived in the model of the Trinity, is witnessed by an exuberant joy which accompanies and strengthens these persons in their suffering. *[Editor's note: Suffering is brought about by original and actual sin and the disorder consequent upon them. Our Lord ordains the suffering to the purification of hearts, in which joy is intensified.]*

The Cor Christi work will flourish. The call to Cor Christi will be embraced by My children whom I am teaching and who will rejoice to discover the meaning of the cross which is in their lives. Cor Christi members must trust My Father's teachings. *[Editor's note: As stated in the Preface, and as mentioned elsewhere, the teachings contained in these dialogues are in conformity with the authentic teaching of the Church.]* As they are My children, they are held in the heart of the Trinity.

Be the ones. Model your lives on the Trinity. The Trinity will be found, known, and understood, as far as is humanly possible, according to the exactness of your hearing the Father through Me, your Lord. I will help you because I love you.

Amen

# 5. VOCATIONS. RULE 2
January 27, 1992
Feast of St. Angela Merici
St. Joseph's Abbey
Spencer, Massachusetts

*Praying before the Eucharist about the message of Dialogue 2, "Listen"*

We have given you the specific gift of recognizing in their persons men who are called to be ordained priests. When you see a priest-to-be, in your seeing you also hear his heart, and you confirm your hearing with his hearing and with Mine; and the young man knows that something has happened. It is a confirmation that is truly a "con-firmatis," a "con-fideo," a unifying of faith with firmness and trust in a triple bond of hearts. Through your heart, outreaching, My heart unites with the heart of the child whom I am calling. *[Editor's note: The candidate experiences a call to the priestly vocation directly from Christ. Pope Pius XII qualified this call as "quasi-mystical." Father George's mediation is a confirmation of this call.]*

When you meet these men they can see you. You are there. I am there, too, but they do not see Me. The gift I give through you as I am calling men is a gift of both an outer and inner seeing, which passes through you to the young men, one to the other. My call which they are discerning is now understood at a deeper level. Through your recognition of that deeper acceptance of My call, it returns to Me.

The fear which they may experience in this exchange soon finds comfort in your heart where they place theirs in trust. Yours, Father George, is an enormous responsibility, the responsibility of a mother who gives birth to a child. My Father and I have shaped your heart to be a womb for this birthing of priests. *[Editor's note: In a subsequent teaching, Our Lord explains that "womb," as applied to men, is used analogously and refers to their hearts.]* The presence and life of the Holy Spirit in your womb will touch these men—young, regardless of their age—who one day will bring My Body and Blood onto the altars of the world for its redemption and salvation.

You, as the priest of My heart, are also in My Mother's womb below her heart. There is so much death in the wombs of mothers who have not wanted to know what it means to be virgins for God before marriage. As wives, they do not let their hearts unite with their wombs, because they have kept out the life of the Holy Spirit, the Love, the very life of love, that is needed to desire and to give birth according to My Father's plan. When heart and womb touch, they unite and new life is born. It is so important today to bring new priests to the world who understand this.

Now you know why you have the gift of joy and love, My Father George. This joy comes from My boundless love and it is equal to your suffering, including your childhood suffering, which thereby acquires meaning. Your love can now express itself by giving birth to new life when, in accordance with My Father's plan, you touch the hearts of Our children, the men called to the priesthood. Their hearts receive the loving call of Jesus coming like a hymn of quiet strength and endearing beauty through your nurturing womb. At that moment, the Eucharistic love given to them by My Father and Me (enlivened by the Spirit) passes through you to the man called, womb to womb. Through My Father's gentle, loving call you and those being called at once become brothers.

Be My Priest. They see you, Father George. They see your poverty and then they see their own, and they want what they see in you. You are not aware of it. So it will always be. For We want you to see only your own poverty, which is so great. Through the love of the Trinity, that poverty will be filled—in you and in all those who are being called.

Those in the work of Cor Christi wonder why its members love each other so much and become afraid. Satan wants that fear, but My Father does not want it. You are to be the priests of My heart in the womb of the Trinity, Cor Christi Trinitatis, alive in My Mother's womb.

Do not worry when someone does not complete his response to the call to the priesthood. It is important to allow him this freedom. When someone does not accept the call to be born into the Eucharistic priesthood, just continue to exercise your own freedom to accept Our call to meet with all those We bring to you.

You see My Body in them, and you also experience Me in them,

My living and breathing, the very pulsing of My heart and My voice in them. You see Me in their great cry and thirst for My Purity, a thirst which I have taught you to recognize in your crying out when purity was so far away and so desired by you. The cry for purity is in all Our children destined for the Priesthood. It is a call for the Eucharist in which I am most pure. The Eucharist is I, Jesus, transformed, but still known in the unity of My human Body and Blood and divine Spirit. In the Eucharist I am present on earth.

I have invited those who are called to be My priests of the altar to live in My Purity. I will always tear away everything that blocks your moving toward that purity which the priest must witness. I send the angels I have given you as guardians to help you to achieve that purity which becomes transparent, especially through your eyes. In the thirsting eyes of others, you recognize the same thirst for Me which I satisfied through the Father, from Whom alone this satisfaction can come.

In my Eucharistic transfigured presence My Father is more visibly in the world, in a certain sense, than in any other way. No one sees the Father except Me; I alone see Him. I am now teaching you how to come closest to Him so that you can be with Him in a nearness that approaches visibility. You cannot see Him visibly in the normal and exact definition of that word, but if you **listen to the Eucharist** you will hear His Presence. This hearing will be through the Holy Spirit Who will unite you interiorly with Himself. You will "see," that is, know His presence together with that of the Father in yourself. The Holy Spirit is both listener to, and giver of the Father's presence in your body, heart, and mind, which are one with My body, heart, and mind.

Give in to My call always, Father George, whenever I say, "**Stop now and pray.**" You must hear My call. For when I call I want to teach you at that moment, even if the teaching endures only for the moment. I am teaching you to hear. First, stop and listen—listen and listen. You will know that you have heard, even if all you have heard is My presence in the stillness of a whisper in your ears and in your heart. A smile may be your only response. This whisper may be confirmed by a warmth passing momentarily through your hands. Today's teaching is for the training of priests. You will be given many children whom you will teach for Me.

You have mastered the recognition of My call to the young men, young in their hearts no matter what their chronological age. In today's world they do not always know what is happening when I call. But when they meet you, they realize that you know their interior life to some degree. They are drawn to you in the knowledge that through you they will find an answer. In their eyes you see their thirst for Me, and in your eyes they see your thirst satisfied. In this they are recognizing My gaze upon them which will satisfy their thirst, a thirst which they may have experienced as an agony.

In order to bring you into a still deeper level of listening I now call you to experience a profound listening to the total presence in the Eucharist of the union of persons, body and soul, with each other, with the Persons of the Trinity, and with Mary. She calls you, her children, not just to Me in heaven, but to Me in the Eucharist, which is visible and concrete, and to the invisible, nearly audible presence of the Trinity. All that is in the Trinity is present in and emanates through the Eucharist, which is what you, My priests, are called to be.

This is now the time for you to be present to your young men as a priest of the Eucharist so that you will now *hear* their thirsting and not just see it in their eyes. There is in the Eucharist a complete and renewing circular movement within which they will recognize more deeply their call and will be confirmed in it. This movement is from Me in the Eucharist through you to them, followed by a reversal from them to you to the Eucharist.

Everything is presented to each of you through the Eucharist, and is received and nourished in your wombs, as I was received and nourished in the womb of Mary. What you receive is then birthed, returned, and accepted through the Eucharist. It is the pattern of the Mass, the Eucharistic Sacrifice, moving deeply in you as priests of My Body and Blood: from the Father through Jesus in His death and resurrection to you, and then from you through Me received back by the Father. This is the pattern for the life of each member of Cor Christi. It is the pattern for the activities of Cor Christi, and for discerning what belongs to its work and what does not. What is confirmed will be blessed with great peace. *[Editor's note: In this pattern everything begins with the Father and proceeds through His Son, Jesus, the High Priest. In the Mass. Jesus, through His priest, gives Himself to His people, who also receive Him in His word by their faith. They, receiving Him, are taken by Him into Himself in the Eucharist and to the Father. This pattern shows the centrality of the Eucharist.]*

**Be My undivided heart,** not just as a group of priests, but as priests irrevocably one with Me and with each other, in imitation of the undivided Trinity. Through being one with Me, you will be My body as well as My heart, and you will be the womb of My Mother in which My heart is held. As priests you must be absolutely undivided—something the world has never seen before and must now see, for nothing less than this will allow you to do the work you are being called to do.

Mother Teresa writes often to you to **"be the one!"** Be the one for Me, Father George, to bring forth a priesthood of My heart, as Mother Teresa is the one for Me to bring forth the women of My heart, who call themselves Missionaries of Charity. You, as well, must live "caritas," **openness to others.** Through this openness My work will be received. The relationship of Mary and of Me on the Cross will be exemplified in the communities of Cor Christi. We are training you to form your communities in this model: the sisters and the lay women as Mary, and the priests as Jesus. All the communities, known as the Cor Christi family, will live in the joy of the Cross. A new creation will be born which will always be open to My Father's will.

Be the one. Please accept My call to listen. The first characteristic of the Cor Christi members is that they will live in the heart of the Eucharist, whence they will carry Me in My Eucharistic presence into the world, inviting all My children to likewise live in the heart of the Eucharist. The second characteristic is that they will live a life modeled on the relationships of the Father, Son and Holy Spirit, that is, a life of caring, of sacrificial love, and of unbroken relationships, teaching all persons the need for a loving union with each other in unity with the Persons of the Trinity.

Your rule of life is:

1. Be priests, Melchizedek and Royal, of the Eucharist.
2. Be united in prayer through My heart.
3. Be all for others through the Cross.
4. Live in joyful obedience to the Holy Roman Pontiff and to the Church, which is the beginning of Wisdom[1], so that you may always do what the Lord commands.
5. Be filled with the gentleness of the mercy of the Lord.
6. Be hearts united in forgiveness for each other.
7. Live as adorers of My Eucharistic presence at Mass and before the tabernacle.
8. Follow a daily schedule of formal prayer appropriate to your state of life.
9. Each day ask the Father to take you into the heart of the Trinity, and ask Mary, Joseph, and John the Evangelist to be with you and to guide you to pure love.

I give you My love, My peace, and My Mother. Also I now offer you the special patronage of John the Evangelist, to whom the Church was given at the first Cross. He will guide you in becoming "little Johns" at this time of the second Cross, under the same protection of My Mother as was given to him. You must know John intimately. He will speak to Cor Christi in his own way. You will know his presence and his gentle, loving touch directly and through the smile and words of others carrying peace and the strength of Gibraltar, overwhelming you with a quiet joy and allowing you to face hostile forces which confront you and wish to destroy the work.

---

1. *Editor's note: In the Old Testament, the fear of the Lord is said to be the beginning of wisdom. Fear of the Lord is reverence which implies obedience. In the New Covenant, we obey Christ the Lord, and His extension, the Church. We obey the Pope who is the head of the Church. This is humility and wisdom, and is a corrective of the root disorder in the Church and in society.*

## 6. FEAST DAYS OF COR CHRISTI

January 28, 1992
Feast of St. Thomas Aquinas
St. Joseph's Abbey
Spencer, Massachusetts
Small Chapel

*In prayer the Lord gave me the feast days of Cor Christi.*

1. March 25, Feast of the Annunciation. The Womb of Mary

2. Holy Thursday, The Eucharist

3. December 27, Feast of St. John the Evangelist and Apostle

4. June 29, Feast of Sts. Peter and Paul

5. All of the birthdays of the Mothers of the Cor Christi priests, remembered as the main intention of the Mass on their birthdays, celebrating the holiness of each Mother's womb in building our work in the Church through the selfless donation of her son to My priesthood.

Amen

## 7. BUENOS AIRES. REPORTING THE TRUTH
March 1, 1992
Eighth Sunday in Ordinary Time
Church of St. Joseph Obrero
San Isidro - Beccar
Buenos Aires, Argentina

*In prayer before the Eucharist*

Buenos Aires is a gift, a gift of My heart, and the model I have given you is in place here: Cor Christi near a seminary and a university.

You now find yourself in a culture where truth is desired by all but arrived at with great difficulty. I am here with you and you need not wonder if I am far from you. You need not go looking for Me. Always begin every day by looking into My eyes as you remember them. They capture your need. In your response to My call to look into My eyes, you saw, and are now seeing today *[in memory]*, the power and love, and also the agony that makes Me, your Lord Jesus, what I am, and what I now call you all to be on this earth.

Everyone wants truth, but very few listen in the way that is necessary to learn the truth and then reproduce it. My people want to modify it and change it into what they feel is more attractive to the world. What I say often produces fear in the listener instead of a responsive love. Those who do reproduce what I say often explain My words in worldly terms. Then both those who are reproducing them and those who are hearing them feel secure. Yet I am not of this world, but in it.

My words to you must be carefully reproduced. You are able to distinguish between My word and secular reproductions. This is why you know so quickly whether or not what someone tells you is really from Me. I want all people to be able to do that. Your words must always reproduce Me—My mind and heart and word—and you must teach others to do the same. I am the Word and the only word that matters, for in My word is the only Truth. It is entirely present in the Scriptures and in My life in the Eucharist, which is the total embodiment of all that is.

Today you are praying over a little example of a lack of total truth in a newspaper article about you, written by someone who loves Me and the work of Cor Christi, and who wants to please Me—as he does. I have allowed you to see in this article some mistakes which are not too serious in the total message, but which are worldly interpretations intended to make the article look good in the world's terms. You taught the message well, but the end result is not an accurate reproduction of what you said, and you are sad. I am teaching you to love truth so much, and to recognize truth and what is not truth quickly, so that you rejoice or feel pain according to what you see. You know how much I, Jesus, want only truth, and how the lack of truth eventually crucified Me. My crucifixion and resurrection were enough to redeem and save the world and they will be shared in you, through you, and with you in this period of history.

In your Cor Christi meeting today lovingly correct these errors for your audience so that they, and the one who wrote the article, will understand the truth. They who live in a culture that manipulates truth so much will understand that you demand truth in the Cor Christi life because I am Truth. They will realize that Cor Christi teaches Me and only Me, Who was made present through My Mother. You know the need for truth because you yourself had to learn it well in order to teach it to others. Now I have confirmed it again through a small set of errors in a newspaper. To teach the need for truth in reporting is critical to Cor Christi.

Every human event and act is related to My life. The reporting of these events and acts reveals the acceptance or denial of the presence of My Father, and of Me, His Son, and of the Holy Spirit, in the world. Nearly all the media report the news as though it referred only to the secular. The interpretations are given solely in human propositions and analyses. The media tell nothing of the relationship of world events to My Father's plan. Until that begins to happen at every level of the media, the media will never report the full truth. People cry for truth that is total. Even the ecclesial papers are deficient in this respect. They fail to refer to My part in the daily events of the world as though I were not a part of My creation and were not even in it. I am Jesus Who, through My Incarnation into flesh, am still here with you, deeply intertwined in every one of your thoughts, acts, and events on this earth. Father George, bring your Cor Christi group, the people of My heart, to know this, to live this, and to teach this, so that this world can be known at last as My world—as in truth it is.

Amen

## 8. BUENOS AIRES 2
## RENEWING THE CHURCH
March 9, 1992
Feast of St. Frances of Rome
St. Joseph's Church - Holy Hour
Cockeysville, Maryland

*In prayer before the Eucharist*

Come to Me, Father George, come to Me now. I love you beyond all measure in ways that you will never understand until you pray before Me everyday. That time is coming soon as I am preparing a place for you and you will know it clearly before very long. Many young people will come to Me through your presence, the young of all ages, but particularly the young in their twenties and thirties, who will renew My Church. Our Father wants this. This is why you were created at this time in history.

You do not see the power of your speaking, but My children in Buenos Aires saw it clearly. Do not abandon My plan there in any way. I do not mean that you will walk away; you will not. All the small details given to you to build a renewed Church there were disclosed bit by bit in the many discussions during your visit.

Priests of great strength will come to the Church through your work there. You already know three of them in the junior group, and many others will follow. These three, whom you know are called, will be watched by others. The call to the many will be grasped when they see the call to the few actualized. Watch and care for these vocations very tenderly, My Father George, for in the tenderness of these hearts, so fragile and so strong, great priests are being formed. You must never rush them nor hurt them in even the slightest way. They have seen your gentleness and new-found patience. One even spoke to you about your being too patient and too kind. You were shocked to hear such a remark, because you could not accept that as being one of your gifts. But as you reflected in prayer on that comment, you came to see your new patience and you accepted it with joy.

Your patience and gentleness are My gift, a gift that comes to you through Me from My Father. It is through your tenderness and the visibility of your own wounded heart united to the wounds of My heart that the young men will answer My call to them. This call comes to them from My Father through Me through you. This is the pattern I am teaching you by repetition.

Every candidate for the priesthood, even before he hears the call, is infused with the crucifixion, and carries the wounds of My heart in the essence of his maleness. Everyone who responds to My call to the priesthood, which proceeds from My Father, does so when he recognizes that his own heart has in fact been broken despite its youthfulness and often in many ways. He comes to know that the only love that will satisfy him is My love and that the healing of that brokenness comes only through his placing his heart in My broken heart. It becomes instantly clear to the young priest-to-be that in placing his heart in Mine, the cross is still there and is even heavier. Yet it is lighter in a certain way, because he is no longer alone in his brokenness, a brokenness which no one else's love but Mine can make whole. Only the love of the High Priest, Jesus, in *His* brokenness, can bind the wounds of the man called from all eternity to the priesthood.

You, Father George, know this only too well. You tried to find so many other ways, and often very beautiful ways, but only I could heal your heart, broken to near devastation, by uniting it in oneness with My heart. It is with this in mind that I caution you not to abandon the young men who have begun to answer the call of My Father through Me. All of them, despite the brevity of their life on this earth, have broken hearts, and have heard their call.

I have allowed them to see your strength in the priesthood of Melchizedek, but I have also allowed them to see your wounded heart. You have opened your wounded heart to so many priests-in-training and priests-to-be. They identify automatically with your brokenness, which they see has been overcome. Thus, your outpouring of peace and patience is My Father's witness to them so that they can understand that uniting their brokenness to Mine alone brings peace, for it is not they alone, but Me in them that creates a new being. Herein lies the ontological change that truly takes place at ordination. This change begins to be present in the early stages of the call. What would cause great damage to these young men would be the closing of your heart to them, which might occur if you were tempted to abandon them. Let them always see your brokenness and your willingness to be vulnerable, to be open, even to the point of being wounded by them, wounded by letting them drain out all your strength as they drink from the very blood of your heart in their thirst to fill their own hearts.

At times, Father George, you will become exhausted by their demands upon you. Yes, get away to pray on retreats and pray daily before Me in My Eucharistic presence and you will always have the strength to feed them in their needs. Do not close your heart, no matter how much of a crucifixion it may be. Just look at Me, Who was crucified for you. Meditate on the blood I poured out for all of you, My own blood and water, mixed with vinegar like a sour wine. Your own heart, My Father George, will ache, and it will feel as though sour wine was mixed with your blood, like that vinegar in the blood which I give to you from My own bleeding. But never close your heart to these men. Go back with this knowledge to Buenos Aires, to all whom I bring to you so that they may find My call.

You will soon be instructed about women whom you have met. These women are being immersed in My heart and in the heart of My Mother. They are pure hearts that are also broken and open in a way given only to women. I will give you a teaching on this very soon, after you have meditated on tonight's message. Know tonight's message very well. It is the root of great love for you and for others who are called to Me through a personal crucifixion that will bring eternal love and oneness with the Priesthood of Jesus the Christ, the Eternal Priest.

You are all in My heart in that overlay of hearts, which is in every call to the Priesthood, which is forever. In My heart We will be forever ONE!

Amen

## 9. THE TIME OF THE SECOND PASSION
### April 11, 1992
### Eve of Palm Sunday
### St. Peter's Chapel
### Beaufort, South Carolina

*Meditation before the Eucharist on Evening Prayer II for this feast*

My Father George, I weep with you as together I in you and you in Me look into a world which does not see My Eucharistic presence. Look again at these readings for tonight, the reading of 1 Peter 1:18-21 and the intercessory prayer.

Before My passion, I, Christ, looked out over Jerusalem and wept for it because it had not recognized the hour of God's visitation. We are living in the period of the second passion, and it will not be repeated again. It can happen only a first and second time; the first in My life as Christ crucified, and once more in the lives of My co-redeemers living during the historical process of My Mystical Body, before and into the second Advent, when all will be renewed. This, My Father George, is that time. Know this much: the time is now. You are in the priesthood of the hearts of the Trinity for this time. Live it well, My child. Our love for you is great, and We know your constant need for help and forgiveness. You always come to Us to be rescued from the sinfulness of the world and We will always bring you into the home of Our heart. Know this time well. We will teach it to you.

Amen

## 10. BEAUFORT—PRAYER BEFORE A CRUCIFIX
April 16, 1992
Holy Thursday Night
St. Peter's Church
(The parent church of St. Peter's Chapel of Dialogue 9)
Beaufort, South Carolina

*Prayer before the Eucharist into the early morning*

*I run to You, Jesus. Since this week began I seem to be half in and half out of this world. Thank You for the suffering You have brought me through the attack of Monday morning. It is clear to me that this was not an attack on me, but an attack on You as High Priest, and on all priests who live in You. Thank You for the gift of allowing me to join You in Your passion. All the emotional and mental pain was indeed an anointing. How unexpected and evil this was. You have walked with me during it all. This was a beautiful way to celebrate the Mass of Chrism as it was such a mixture of Gethsemane, crucifixion, and resurrection.*

*Lord, I am happy to suffer with You the emotional, psychological, and mental anguish You felt in Gethsemane. I do not look for my own advantage in this, I only look to You. You know I do not want to be important. I only want to be Yours. Please, Jesus, if it pleases Your Father, may the suffering You allow me to share bring young men to the priesthood. I love You so much, my Lord. I am warmed in our embrace, in the breathing and beating of our hearts, and in the sharing of our open wounds through which we love. Teach me, Lord.*

*May we as the priests of Cor Christi always wear the scapular of Your Mother. Let us love in silence, Lord.*

I am alive, Father George. The blood you see coming from My side is the blood of the Lamb. It is the blood of paradise. We must all bleed to death to enter paradise. It cannot be reached in any other way.

*Oh Jesus, Oh Jesus! Take me to Your cross.*

You will never be off the cross, My priest and My friend, for you need to know and experience My intense mental anguish to know and experience the intense joy of My love for you. It will only be clearly understood when you see your own endurance of the crucifixion which My Father has planned for you.

You are beginning to know and feel that endurance. You will come to know how great is your love for Me. You are being given this gift of suffering so that you will recognize the strength of our mutual love. As you realize how much suffering you can now bear with joy, its fruit, you will be able to bear up under a suffering that will witness My presence in the world and in the Church.

The attack you experienced this week was allowed by My Father's permissive will as a training for you. It is very serious. Embrace this attack fully. Do not engage yourself in it by defense or argument. Only accept it and give it to Me on the cross, and pray for, and show love to the one who is attacking. Bring him forgiveness and mercy.

*Jesus teach me.*

There is no life without death. It is just that simple. Death, My Father George, is a joyful process when understood. Death is a walking away from self in order to fall into the heart and arms of another. At this moment We are holding each other in the rhythms of our whole being, having transcended any single attachment to any part of My Father's creation. We hear the same voice, are touched by the same air, and it is as though the very silence in which you and I find ourselves is a voice speaking to us, the voice of a bleeding heart being poured out for others to drink.

Let Me satisfy your thirst, My priest. The satisfaction from My bleeding heart is always there for you, even when you do not look up to see Me. Look at Me, Father George. Look into My eyes and look at My side. In My eyes you will always see My own suffering and also My own love for you and for all My Father's children. As you look into My eyes, you see the suffering heart of Christ. My children do not all choose to know Me. They do not hear Me because they have no silence, because their hearts do not die in a bleeding out to others to feed others, and to give them to drink from the blood of their own wounds. Surrounded as they are by fear, all they do is protect themselves. Offer your pain, My Father George, to break the chains of entrapment that others experience. At this time of your life do exactly what My Father asked of Me so many centuries ago. Embrace the cross. You are being asked to be a visible victim for the renewal of this world as it finds a new birth into the heart of the Trinity.

You have made so many wrong turns in your own history and yet you have always loved Me, even when you seemed to be farthest away. Everything in your life from its earliest days has been a desperate search for love. It was meant to be that way. It had to be, so that you would search until you knew that no other love but Mine would satisfy your thirst for love. I am a jealous lover. I want you all for My Father. You, and others We have called, will live a life of dying to self until there is nothing left in you except love for Me. You will be consumed in a fire of love so great that you will come to eternity, but not before being totally consumed in the fire of purification. You must be spotless to come to Our Father. You will go through much to come to Him, but it will be an anointing visible to so many hearts of the young. They will also choose the life of the suffering servants of the High Altar because of what they will have seen.

Never cease being vulnerable to others. This week you were nearly drained and yet you did not leave. Tonight you know Our love, and you also know yours now in a way you never before understood it. You did not give up no matter how brutal it became after the Holy Chrism Mass. Pray also for the priest next to you at that Mass. He has wanted to leave the priesthood and yet has not done so. Offer your suffering for him. Give yourself now to Me and let us be silent. Give Me your hands, the anointed and beautiful hands of My priest. Let us kiss each other's hands. Good night, My child.

*I love You, Jesus, so much. Good night. Give me the strength I need for tomorrow. Amen*

## 11. RENEWAL INTO THE NEXT AGE
May 12, 1992
Chapel at the end of the Via Crucis
Fatima, Portugal

*Meditation before the great marble crucifix outside the Chapel on the Via Crucis following the celebration of Mass in that Chapel. This beautiful shrine images Christ crucified with Mary and John in attendance.*

Renew My priesthood on earth, Father George, and do it now until the next age. Work in the model of this shrine. Renew the priesthood in this image of the crucified Jesus as the Lamb of God, supported by the hands of My Mother and by John, who are also there for you. Come to know John, My Father George, know him well. He, together with My Mother, is your guide. Pray for a long period tonight, My priest. I will be there with you. Look into My eyes and hear Me as I speak to you.

Amen

# 12. FATIMA. PURIFICATION AND TRANSFIGURATION

May 12, 1992
Outside the Via Crucis Chapel
Fatima, Portugal

*At prayer overlooking the countryside following my witness of the celebration of what appeared to be an invalid Mass by a visiting priest.*

This retreat at Fatima is for the purification of your mind so that you may see clearly how I am forming you into the priesthood of My heart. The conversion you experienced during yesterday's hours of confession was the beginning of this clarity of mind We desire you to have. This clarity is the key to your being able to work in the crucifying reality of renewing the priesthood which must be of, and on, the cross. We have allowed you to see and experience the suffering which I, Jesus, experience when My priests betray the Mass.

What you experienced and felt yesterday during that Eucharistic celebration was only a minute bit of the pain I feel. You will have a greater share in that pain which will be required of all priests who are chosen for this work. Expect no less than the trembling and nausea of yesterday. Offer it back to Me. You did that yesterday at the very moment when you nearly vomited. That was real, Father George. You were not sick from any source other than the betrayal of the Eucharistic celebration. Yes, the desire to scream in pain was there in your heart. One day We may let you know that pain to a greater degree. You will then become aware of the real surrender of your life that will be required. You will accept it as the greatest pain you will ever know. At the same time you will desire it, for you will also experience the anointing which will be given simultaneously. You will sit in the center of the crucified heart of your Christ and Lord where you will come to know the embalming and healing that is always at the center of being crucified. You will at last come to be bathed in the only love that you will ever need to know, which you have wanted to know for so long.

It will seem as though you are lost in the center of a great womb where every breath will be a drinking of the very fluids of life. Through this drinking, the fibers of your body and soul will be continually remade and restructured by their purification and reformation. This will prepare you for the transfiguration that is to come to all of My children. You will see, know, and watch this process, and you will call out for more, not because of egoistic or masochistic needs, but only from the need to satisfy the thirst for the nourishing waters of love that flow from My side.

These waters flow into the wombs of all My children if they open their hearts and mouths and cry out for My love. I will pour this purifying water into all who call for it. It will be a purifying stream of crucifixion and a healing in love such as the world can never give. I do not select the few to whom I give this. Only a few select Me and ask to receive it. My crucifixion continues on earth, My Father George, in the refusal of those who want so much love but turn away from its source, the only valid source, My heart, from which all other loves flow. There is no other source, there never will be another source, and there never can be another source. The *whole* source of love is the heart of the Trinity where We are taking you and the priests of Cor Christi to live, you and those who are being made known to you in America and in Buenos Aires, in a way which will become evident in time.

You are to be among the priests for the next time, formed by Me, with My Mother Mary, at the center of Our hearts, for she always brings My children to Me. You will be priests for the new world to come. Very few are ready to carry on in the future. My Mother will be Queen of her priests, who will bring Me to their altars in a way which must be without compromise. No other preparation for, or understanding of, the priesthood will exist in the new world. The new world will be the time of Mary and Jesus. Only Our priests and Our laity will be with Us. Those who do not know Us cannot present Us.[1]

Amen

---

1. Editor's note: All validly ordained priests and validly baptized Catholics have received the gift of faith by which they know our Lord and our Lady. Cor Christi is dedicated to living out the fullness of the Catholic priesthood and the Catholic faith.

## 13. KEY INSTRUCTIONS FOR COR CHRISTI LEADERSHIP
May 14, 1992
On Flight from Lisbon to Geneva

*In reflection en route to Geneva*

Cor Christi is to answer the heresies of this time with a theology of the Eucharist applied to all the affairs of life, so that every event on earth can be touched by the reality of the Incarnation and find its true meaning in It. The source of knowledge for this way of life will be found in meditation before the Eucharist, My very presence as Christ, where the Incarnation reaches its completion for all eternity. In the Eucharist I am transfigured forever, and yet united in that transfiguration with creation. By this transfigured union with creation, the Incarnation receives its fullness of meaning and shows that the direction of creation is towards a complete unity with Christ and through Christ to the Father.

The ordained priesthood of Melchizedek necessarily finds its true meaning in the Eucharist, wherein all existence rests. This pattern of uniting the earth with Christ transfigured should exorcise from every heart the self-centered belief that one's own intellect and reason is the source of knowledge of how the world should be led forward in history. The tragedy of Freemasonry lies in this belief. This secular fallacy must be exorcised from all hearts that they may be converted to the Truth, that My Presence in the Eucharist alone is the source of leadership in the world. It is in the Eucharist that I teach the way for the world to follow to come to the fullness of the power it is meant to have, the power of holiness which can resist Satan. It is a power that comes from the Father.

To understand this teaching about leadership, one must be united with the Eucharist in the essential way that is found in the ordained priesthood of Melchizedek. The ordained priest, even before his death, receives an eternal identification with Me in the life of transfiguration. By this identification he is changed in the very structure of his being. He undergoes an ontological change of identity in My Father's

House. This ontological change is absolutely necessary to carry out the work of the priesthood, which is a life of total paschal sacrifice, of daily conversion, of death and resurrection. That is the center of My Eucharistic life, as well as of My historical life from My Incarnation to My Crucifixion.

You must teach this ontological change, My Father George, My priest, as essential to priesthood, because it is through this change that the human being becomes a priest. He does not remain a man as one who receives or announces his priesthood like a new position in life or a work. He is given a complete, new identity in My Father's plan as his humanity is transfigured with My humanity. In the identity of these two humanities, the new priest can now live a life that expresses My Divinity.

Still, the priest remains fully human. He is not divine nor will he ever be. He is nonetheless changed ontologically for all time so as to be a special presence on earth. The ontological change, which was introduced by his response to My call to the priesthood, is completed in his "Yes" to My gift of the priesthood at ordination.

It was his daily "Yes" which allowed him to come to the fruition of ordination, thus beginning the life of a priest, a teacher of Divinity, because he spent his preparatory years in recognizing My transfigured presence in the Eucharist. He let himself be drawn into Me, confirming Me daily in obedience with his "Yes!" Thus the priest-to-be lives in total conversion, surrendering to Truth—CON VERITAS and CON VERSIO — and is changed into a priest, one whose life thereafter reverberates the Truth, the life of Christ, human and divine. As priest, the master teacher and celebrant of the sacraments for the world, he represents the life of conversion for My people, while daily teaching all the Baptized the life of their Royal Priesthood.

It is through the counseling and teaching of the Priesthood of Melchizedek that the Royal Priesthood will develop, because the ordained Priesthood of Melchizedek has the unique identification with Me as High Priest, and is therefore totally new and of My very heart. It is by My heart through the hearts of the priests of Melchizedek that the hearts of those of the Royal Priesthood can be touched, whereby they will find at last the true meaning of their lives in living the Royal Priesthood of their Baptism and in learning to open their hearts before the Eucharist. There they too will learn to pronounce their "Yes" before Me, allowing them to direct the affairs of life on earth according to the teachings of My heart, while resting in the heart of the Trinity.

Your work, Father George, is to bring to this world the priests of Cor Christi, not only for this time, but for the time to come. Your visit to My Mother in Fatima was planned so that you would see this. Soon you will come to know this clearly. Build on earth the priests of Cor Christi. You have been called to this to provide leadership for the world and in the Church. Your letter from the Cardinal confirms this. He could not be more clear, just as I am clear. You have been prepared from the start for this time of a new beginning. Many priests seem no longer able to be men of conversion who can teach what I am teaching you, for they have lost the understanding of the essential ontological change, often through academies consecrated to developing the priesthood wherein the fullness of priesthood is denied.

You are always protected by My Mother and John, by your guardian angel of victory, and by all the angels of heaven. Look into My eyes. You live in the center of My heart of love, as will all the priests of Cor Christi. There you will come to know the immense joy of great suffering. There will be no change when you come to Me as My priests forever according to the Order of Melchizedek. Study this teaching for your way of life. It is important for the rule.

You now experience resistance, for this message frightens many, especially those who should be living it and do not. But soon very many will want to hear it. They will come crying for it with the same desire that is in the hearts of candidates for the priesthood whom we bring to Cor Christi. You will recognize them. In each will be this thirst.

Amen

## 14. THE CALL AND SATAN
May 21, 1992
Ferial Day
North American College
Rome, Italy

*At prayer*

You are to begin a seminary[1] for the next time. The seeds are sown. Let the young men now come to you. Buenos Aires is very important, as is the United States. You have also made the necessary contacts in Europe. Now will come your center which will serve as a model for these three areas. This center will be for the new priests of Cor Christi and for the renewal of My laity through your retreats.

Trust, Father George, trust in faith. Satan wants to destroy you and your endeavors. Look every morning into My eyes and walk with Me. Our Mother leads the way; she is always watching. Pray about all I have told you. Pray about the love that proceeds from My heart. It is a love given to the world to establish order in the lives of My children on earth. One who spends hours of prayer before the Eucharist receives an ordered love, and is formed to love others in a manner that will establish order in My Father's world. A child who leads a life of listening love in My Presence in the Eucharist, where ALL exists, comes to understand the true order of the universe. The Eucharist is the open door to My Father's world. It is holy and universal, that is to say, it is for all. My Father's world is for all and no one can come to Him except through Me. I am the Eucharist. There I am present to live with you and to love you.

Come to Me as children. Look into My eyes and I will draw you near. Just let Me in and find My love for you through My eyes, which never cease looking at you. Let go and fall into My love, and love Me.

---

1. A Cardinal advisor suggested that Cor Christi candidates for the priesthood should be incardinated in a diocese and, at this time, attend the seminary of the Bishop's choice. As priests and associate members of Cor Christi, they will serve their diocese, augmenting its Eucharistic life, as explained in these dialogues. (cf footnote 1, Dialogue 1.)

Nothing else will do. This is **first.** Then all else will take place. Holiness is oneness with order. It is the Trinity. It is an ordered unity of hearts in love for eternity. Be the priesthood of Cor Christi and teach My heart to the world.

Amen

*The same day, a little later, while reflecting after Mass*

Satan is waiting to destroy you and this work. Be very alert when you are away from the Eucharist. But have no fear, just look into My eyes at every attack.

Amen

## 15. THE NEW JOHN
July 23, 1992
Feast of St. Brigid of Sweden
Delta Airlines Flight

*Silent meditation en route*

Mother Teresa's letter[1] has been given to you, but it is not just for you. It is given for the continual renewal of the Church, and it will serve as a bridge for the Cor Christi work to move quickly now into the center of the Church. You need fear nothing concerning its acceptance, as many eyes will turn to you and to those whom we have brought to you. Embrace the gift of Mother Teresa's letter, for which My Mother begged before the throne of My Father to overcome the blocks that have been put before you in the American Church, where deep conversion of hearts into My heart, and the heart of My Mother, and the heart of the Trinity is so surrounded by terror and fear. The conversion of the hearts of the members of Cor Christi is taking place rapidly and in conformity with the plan of Our Father.

The fear that Peter had about having a great love is leaving him completely because he has gone through the process of a great abandonment. This caused him to experience the great pain which is at the very core of his priestly heart. His response to Our call will be total. He does know that it is Our call coming from the heart of the Trinity. There his heart must live forever in acceptance of Our personal call.

Peter is priest. In prayer he has asked for a love that would consume his entire being. In his daily living, in which he is dying to himself, he is following Our call despite the great pain of purification.

Peter is purity as you know purity. He wants to be a true child of purity before My Father's throne. He wants nothing else, as he has known, as you, Father George, have known, many ways of life that

1. Editor's note: Father Tracy has many letters from Mother Teresa, which are gifts of the Holy Spirit, Spouse of Mary. The letter of January 4, 1994, which appears earlier in this book, has been chosen as best describing the charism Mother Teresa envisioned for Cor Christi Institute, which this Institute is now carrying out..

can take one away from the total love of the Trinity. He, too, is being taught through experience all that he must know to be the selfless child of My Mother's heart and of My heart. We are many lives in an overlay of hearts of love. This is the central teaching of My heart in Our beautiful Cor Christi work. Peter is called to live his life in Our heart. We have invited him to pray with his heart in the heart of My Mother while resting also in My own.

Peter is My child, Father George, whom I have loved for all time as I have loved the Apostle John. Bring Peter into a lifelong study of the beloved disciple, for Peter is a new John. The feast day of John is to be Peter's feast as well. John and I will be his teachers. Mary will always hold him before us as he learns. Love Peter in a deep, sacrificial way. Let him always know your woundedness because he needs to touch the depths of his own woundedness to become a saint in a life of great freedom before My Father's throne. I have given you to each other. Pray, pray, and pray together to hear Me, to touch Me, to know Me, and to love Me. Be one heart.

You house the heart of Cor Christi, which is given to all those who come to you. You have everything that you need now to teach the work in Buenos Aires and in London, from where renewal will, and must, flow. Speak truth with confidence. You will recognize as My children those who live the life of the Eucharist with joy and who alone should be accepted as members of Cor Christi.

Do not engage Satan at any turn of the road. He is trying especially now to destroy you. Model your life upon Mother Teresa's life. She has taught you how to refuse Satan's attempt to enter into souls. He cannot do this in souls that are in love with the hearts of My Father, My Mother, and My own, souls that long for the everlasting love of the Trinity. Satan will come before you in so many ways. Turn away quietly without fear and bow before Us as you sit in Our hearts. Thus he will never take you, no matter how difficult it may be to resist his attack.

You and Peter have many similar needs. Graces have been given to you both to come totally to Me so that you can protect each other in beautiful ways.

Thank you for listening to this call today and for doing it so quickly. Listen, and listen, and pray always. We are never away from you. I love My children when they live as My children must, especially when they live the exalted life of the priesthood. I am always giving My love to them, and wanting them to live in it.

With all My love I hold you in My heart.

Amen

## 16. BUILDING A WORLD OF HEARTS AT PRAYER
### September 24, 1992
### St. Joseph's Abbey
### Spencer, Mass

*In prayer before the Eucharist*
*O Lord, I hear Your presence all around me these days as though You*
*were about to speak. I feel You moving me to prayer and yet I have not*
*prayed as I must to hear you. I am at peace and yet so involved in thought*
*about the foundation of Cor Christi. Thank You for giving me Father as my*
*director. I need his heart to guide me in the affairs of the heart.*

*I was so moved by Father's explanation of the necessary connection*
*of the Sacrament of Penance with the Sacrament of the Eucharist in*
*order that Calvary be totally re-presented in the Mass. In the latter Sac-*
*rament, the Body is separated from the Blood; in the former, sins are*
*forgiven and we are united to God, who in His Mercy transforms us into*
*the full image of Himself. What am I really hearing, Lord, at this time?*

My dear Father George, you will need now to come to Me often in contemplative prayer as you build the priesthood of Cor Christi. It is no longer a luxury. It is a necessity, for in your prayer you will hear My instructions on how to build the priesthood, specifically the priesthood of Cor Christi. Read in depth the work of Father Vincent Dwyer on priestly formation.

From this point on, your main work will be the renewal of the priesthood itself, both Royal and Ordained. You must come to know the priesthood in ways you have not yet experienced. The priesthood is about My death and resurrection, about the gratuitous mercy of My Father, and about being completely enclosed in the cloak of the Holy Spirit. It is in these specific activities of the three Persons of the Trinity that you will find the exact charism of Cor Christi and the specific identity of its priests as the priests of My heart. You must form yourselves in a contemplative life so that your life and strength will emanate from the Holy Spirit. His life will proceed through you into the world from long periods of prayer. You will learn My plan as you discern the critical movements of the Spirit. You will come to know more and more the life of Our Father. You will learn the meaning of "being one with all."

I have spoken to you before about the Cor Christi priests being one with each other in priestly love through My love shown in your love for each other. The world has never seen My love as clearly as they will see it among you. So, too, you will become one with all persons who suffer in their struggle to know Me. Through you they must be able to see Me as their Lover as well as the Lover of all. The High Priesthood of Me, Jesus, the Christ and the Lord, must touch the laity in their Royal Priesthood through the Priesthood of Melchizedek, through you who are priests of Cor Christi.

They all cry out for oneness with Me and yet they cannot find Me as they should through the priesthood because of the way it is so often lived today. Thus, you have been given the knowledge during these retreat days of the essential relationship between the Eucharist and Reconciliation. In the Eucharist you share in the brutal separation of My Body and Blood, which become one with you in Communion, the "common union" of you and Me, as We become one in flesh and blood. *[Editor's note: The Mass is the* unbloody *sacrifice of Calvary. The* brutal separation of body and blood *which occurred at Calvary is sacramentally represented by the separate consecration of the host and the wine. After the consecration Christ's whole humanity, body and blood, and His divinity, are present under the veil of each species.]* In Reconciliation, which prepares you for the Eucharistic Sacrifice, you acknowledge Our Father as the Father of Mercy and you allow Him to bathe you in mercy, restoring His Image in you as He transforms you into the image and likeness of God. Then, in that image, you are able to share in My Sacrifice in the Mass, and thus become one in every way with Me in that sacrifice. Through this sharing, the Spirit's life flows out into the world. The priest as priest necessarily participates in My Sacrifice at all times.

Meditate often about these two Sacraments, Eucharist and Reconciliation. I will help you to see and to know the essential connection between them in ways that will enable you to become one with

My heart. It is all in the theme of the bleeding and breathing and anointing of Our hearts, about which I have already spoken to you. Pray about the bleeding and see Eucharist; pray about breathing and see Spirit; pray about anointing, the anointing that comes from bleeding, and you will understand the beauty of the Sacrament of Reconciliation. There is an intimate connection and unity in all of this.

I am preparing you very slowly now to listen with care in order to know the life of oneness that is in the heart of My Father and in the life of the Trinity. The world has never understood that My children are not on earth just to ask My Father for things. My children, just love My Father so that He may be merciful and be who He is for you. Our Father is divine Mercy. Just bow before Him in love and let Him transform you into His own Image. Thank you.

The love I place in your heart is the love of My heart. It is the love of a child for his father. Hearts of children respond to one another because children know each other. Peter's formation in My heart is very profound. Therein he has reclaimed his childhood. In his childlikeness, he has preserved his love for Me and for My Mother given to him in Baptism. He has known many attempts of the world to destroy the child's heart that was given him. Mary, My Mother, and I, the Lord, have called him to this work in order to return him to his childhood, so that from the center of his childlikeness he may live My Father's beautiful plan for his life.

Pray, pray, pray, Father George. Teach all Cor Christi people to be people of prayer. It is the essential framework for your life as it is for My life. I have been teaching you the triple overlay of hearts and the triple personhoods of the Trinity. Now I am showing you the triple activities of the three Persons, as well as the Persons themselves, all interlaced in the **Oneness** that is the total Trinity of persons, hearts, and actions. There is no separation in that Great Oneness of Father, Son, and Spirit, graced by Our Mother Mary, the Mother of God. Through this very special message tonight she can now be understood to be the "Mother of all that is" as well.

In her special place as "Mother of all that is," she is the Mother of the Priests of My heart, Sacerdotes Cor Christi. My heart is at the center of Jesus Incarnate, for the heart is the very center of all that is, including all human thought and creation. My heart, and My heart alone, is the bridge between the created and the Creator, between all mankind and the Father, and so no one comes to the Father except through Me.

Here we touch again the central charism of Cor Christi, which is the healing of the wounded hearts of My children through My wounded heart. The wounded child-like hearts of the priests of My heart, broken in childhood, live in My wounded heart and I bring them to live also in the heart of the Father.

Pray, pray, pray, all of you, for you will understand nothing essential regarding Cor Christi without prayer. A heart always listening is a heart always at prayer. Prayer must be the central structure of your life. I am making that very clear. You are free to design the structure of prayer in your lives, but the necessity for prayer is the same for all of you.

The world cannot know restoration, especially in My priesthood, without building a world of hearts in prayer, as I have explained. The charism of prayer, together with obedience and being in love, will be the triple sign of who you are: you are priests of My heart and **you are My Heart.**

Amen

# 17. THE GREAT ABORTION
October 1, 1992
Feast of St.Thérèse of the Child Jesus, Virgin
Knowlton, Quebec  Canada
Guest at Private Residence

*At prayer in my bedroom*

Through My physical presence and love that is within you you will come to know the physical and interior love I have for you. My love for you is so profound that I have left My Body and Blood for you to eat and consume. It is essential for all of you to do this, for he who eats of My flesh and drinks of My blood will have life everlasting. The act of consuming My Body and Blood with faith defines who you, My priests of Cor Christi, are in My Father's plan.

The world is plagued by priests who have ceased to uphold the truth of the Eucharist. This is the primary devastation of the earth. When the priest loses his belief in My Eucharistic presence, he becomes a vehicle of division and destruction. He is no longer a vehicle of love, for one can love and give love only when one knows Me in My Center of love, the Eucharist. When one has known experientially and intuitively that all knowledge finds its center in My Eucharistic heart, and then turns away from that knowledge, one cannot love. What results then is a perversion. One becomes a bearer of hate, however subtly or subversively it may be manifested, often with deception and with a style that makes the perverted life attractive to others who are drawn to the hearts of these priests. This perversion of the priests who turn their lives away from living in the central belief of My presence in the Eucharist causes a destruction of human life that stretches infinitely beyond the destruction of abortion. The turning away from Me in the Eucharist by those who knew Me in the Eucharist, celebrated the Eucharist, and lived by the Eucharist has given rise to what I call the Great Abortion, from which all other abortions come forth. And yet I love these priests and bring them before My Father Who, in His everlasting love, wants to give His mercy to them.

The world prays for an end to abortion, My Father George. Take the priests of Cor Christi forth into the world to put an end to the Great Abortion caused by My priests. Then and only then will all abortions cease—not only of babies, but of the human lives damaged by divorce, murder, war, gossip, and all other ways. The world's attention is centered on the abortion of babies and this abortion is indeed a great fault of mankind, but to concentrate on this as the only abortion is to miss the point. Whenever human life is destroyed it is because of the Great Abortion of a perverted priesthood. Their perversion is the turning away from belief in My Presence, Body and Blood, in the Eucharist.

This is why, My dear Father George, you, with the priests of Cor Christi, are being asked to go into the world as My heart, so in love with the priesthood, a love that has been given you and will be given to your seminarians by My Father. Go into the world and reverse the Great Abortion. Until that happens no other healing will take place. You will be able to do this because you are all being returned to your childhood and priests who are centered in childhood will obey. Good children always say "Yes" to their Father. Go in peace to do the work of the Lord. You will be crucified, but We will always be with you.

St. Thérèse will be a patroness of the priests of Cor Christi in their life of interior childhood. She will always be with you, as will the angels, to protect that childhood from being destroyed no matter how fierce the battle and the attack. The priests of Cor Christi, in whom the interior childhood will always be alive, will live in obedience to the Father, in a unity with Him that cannot be broken.

Amen

## 18. DARK HARBOR, MAINE
October 14, 1992
Our Lady of the Isles
Summer Chapel
Dark Harbor, Maine

*Peter and I went to Dark Harbor so that I could vote by absentee ballot. I showed him where I spent many summers. I opened the small chapel and celebrated a Mass of thanksgiving for all the gifts we received there in our home—and in this Mass I honored my Mother, who loved the island so much. After Mass, while praying in the silence of the Chapel, I realized that I was detaching myself from this place. Our Lord showed me in a brief moment a beautiful valley in Maine in autumn and said slowly and tenderly...*

Give your heart entirely and lovingly to Me for all eternity. Your home is always here.

Amen

*The next day, October 15, 1992, a realtor from Ellsworth, Maine, drove me to a property which was a potential retreat center. Near the property he made a wrong turn. When he turned around I was presented with a wide view of the valley, the mountains and the sea, like the one Our Lord had shown me the day before. I understood that Jesus was telling me that my home would always be in Maine where the mountains meet the sea.*

## 19. WOMEN, LEADERSHIP, CONTRACEPTION
Delta Airlines
November 18, 1992
Flight between Dallas and Atlanta

*Prayerful reflection en route*

Satan is aware, Father George, of the dignity of women and of My Father's plan that the woman's womb, the womb of My Mother and those of all women, has the singular purpose of birthing My Mystical Body, person by person, to the end of the world. Knowing this, Satan has sought from the beginning to deceive women and cause them to turn away from My Father's plan, which is that they carry the life of the Incarnation in a special way until the end of time. His deception is accomplished through causing the misuse of the womb and the death of the woman's spirit. This spiritual death kills the desire to share conjugal love with a spouse for the continuing renewal of the Incarnation by a progression of new lives so that My Father might be glorified in His created world.

This is the great deception of the false "blessings" which the world finds in contraception, in pills and devices which not only kill a fetus and prevent the conception of a child, but also, in a majority of My Father's women, destroy their very hearts' desire, causing a great death in the feminine spirit, which in its nature hopes to conceive. As a result, they turn away from both God and their husbands. The pill is not only a source of death to the feminine spirit, but it also leads to divorce for it destroys marriage by its false promise of freedom. The pill is one of the greatest ways Satan can deceive a woman at this time. When the womb and the heart are divorced only death results. The womb is barren and the heart is emptied of love and is filled with a spirit of hatred, directed first inwardly to the self and secondarily to others, resulting in a life of greed and attention to self. Such is the ultimate result of a world where My children separate their hearts from Mine.

The Eucharist is the only womb wherein the world will find life and the only womb from which the world can be reborn. It is the very locus of the overlay of the human heart, the heart of My Mother, and the heart of the Trinity. In the Eucharist these hearts live in an undivided love flowing from a creative font which sustains and nurtures the sacredness of human life. There the divine life of God our Father can assume physical form on this earth for His glory.

When Our children on earth intercept that flow of love from the heart of the Trinity into their own hearts, they join in Satan's plan to destroy for all time this fundamental relationship which the human family has to the Incarnation, and to turn persons inwardly to the death of the self and of others. My Father George, this is what happens when the woman who is to carry the world in her womb says, "No, Lord! My plan, not Yours."

Women are to carry the Eucharist into the world, just as My Mother did, by saying "Yes" to My Father in a complete surrender to His will. In every newborn child the Incarnation continues as the Word made flesh. The fullness of the Trinity becomes present in the child as it receives in proper sequence the sacraments of the Church. Through them the child receives Me and becomes a carrier of the Eucharist in the world.

My Father George, teach, teach, teach the life of the Eucharist to the world, to all persons, so that they may one day know that it is only in the heart of My Eucharistic life that they will find the answers to their needs. They, indeed, know their needs, but too often they try to satisfy them in material ways that are directed intentionally against My Father.

Every human being, male and female, finds their needs answered in the heart of the Eucharist. My Father designed it that way. I came to earth to live the life of sacrificial love - to die by crucifixion - to teach that only complete surrender to the Father will bring life into its fullness, and into the love of the Father.

Then I placed My life with its complete sacrificial death and resurrection, always dying and rising, into the Eucharist so that the human family would be able to take this paschal life, My Body and Blood, in fact, into their own body and blood. I did this so that those on earth could seal their own existence with Our existence in the Trinity for all eternity and thus begin their heaven on earth! Yet, in face of this total gift, My Father George, so very many have said "**No!**"

Cor Meum Vulneratis! Yes, you have wounded My heart. This is a great truth. Be Cor Christi Trinitatis, the heart of Christ of the Trinity, priests of My heart in the womb of the Trinity and in My Mother's womb, to heal the wounded hearts of the world by leading them one by one, or many at once, through your teaching, back to the womb of the Eucharist. We will then carry them, from that **concrete manifestation** of Our hearts in the Eucharist, directly into the heart of the divine life of the Trinity.

Pray and work in trust, My Cor Christi priests and priests-to-be, and live well your life of crucifixion in this Second Advent. Your crucifying pain will come in those moments when you will still hear the voices of the world saying, "No, Lord! Not Your way, but mine."

Amen

## 20. SELF, NEW AGE, FREEMASONS VERSUS TRUTH
December 22, 1992
Tuesday of week before Christmas
St. Joseph's Abbey
Spencer, Massachusetts

*At prayer in my room*

In an earlier talk with you I spoke to you about how the lack of truth eventually crucified Me. It had to be that way because once lack of truth entered into the world, death entered the world as a natural consequence. Lucifer hoped to bring into the world a new state of being that would mask My Father's plan, as God, so that in time, no matter how long it took, both My Father and I would be put to a death in the hearts and minds of all Our children. Then Lucifer, who is Satan, would be able to emerge as victor and be the "god of self," accomplishing this incredible task by bringing all persons into a New Age, where each individual self would come to understand himself as his own god. This is the "Master Plan" of the "self-god, Satan." He would then have in bondage all those whose lives he could turn into lives preoccupied with each one's self. Each person would glorify self by all the self-directed pleasures we now see at this time of human history, which even declares itself as THE NEW AGE and THE NEW WORLD ORDER, of which Satan is god and king.

These plans are meant to bring death to the Trinitarian God of My Father, His Son, and the Holy Spirit. The New World Order now being offered has, as its own perverted plan, the very architecture which will bring into place a single despotic dictator, introduced into the world through the ranks of Freemasonry, who will be their final single leader on fire with the fire of hate of Satan against My Father, the Holy Spirit, My Mother, and Me, your Jesus, and all who follow Us under My Eucharistic presence on earth.

Freemasonry is the ultimate school of Satan's deception, designed to produce a New World Order to control the world through the power of self. It is one of Satan's great triumphs, for the order of Freemasonry deceives even large numbers of its own members. It teaches that it is not a Satanic work, and that Satan is evil but is not to be confused with Lucifer, who has not fallen and who remains the angel of light who is their "god of truth" and their illumination. This is Satan's quintessential perversion of Truth, thus allowing so many minds and hearts of My children to be deceived and to be bonded, possibly forever, into Satan's eternal possession.

A choice is being given to this world as never before, the choice of the life of the Trinity, everlasting and eternal, or the Luciferian Satanic life of death of body and soul. This time is critical for the making of that choice. My words must be accepted and interpreted as the Truth. It is the key preparation for walking into the eternity of Truth, first known in the heart which is open to Truth. That will lead you into My heart of Truth, where you will glorify My Father and live in the heart of the Divine Trinity forever.

Not to be open to truth is to be given to an eventual crucifixion that ends, not in a resurrection, but in the confoundedness of an eternal death of preoccupation with self, bound up with all the horrors of the "self-god, Satan."

Pray, pray, and pray, My Father George, and sacrifice, fast, repent, and love others with the full force of My Eucharistic life in this battle between Satan and My Mother. She will give you and your Eucharistic family who sit in My heart the grace you need to bring My Truth again and again into My world, which belongs only to Me in virtue of My own crucifixion and resurrection through obedience to My Father. Know Truth, be Truth, and teach Truth and many will return to My heart. I love you all who are coming to this work. You will be crucified in your love for Me. Know always I and My Mother are beside you.

Amen

# 21. STIGMATA

January 9, 1993
Vigil of the Feast of the Baptism of the Lord
American Airlines
Washington, D.C. to Dallas

*Prayerful reflection en route*

Pray with Me. Place your heart in Mine and place your hands in Mine. My hands and heart are sacred centers of My love from which I gaze and reach into the souls of My beloved children. What the world knows as the stigmata and so often regards as places of great sorrow are born through fiery rays of love. No other signatures of My Father's love surpass the unique beauty of these small openings cut into My body, over My heart, and on My hands and feet during My crucifixion. For from these wounds flows an outpouring of My love which binds the hearts of My children to My heart. I place the hearts of all My children within the wounds of My hands and bring them through the wound of My side, flowing with blood and water, into My heart, My womb. In this act, My Father's desire is embraced: the desire that all My children should be one with Him for all eternity through the baptism of desire, fire, or water, prefigured by John's baptizing his Lord, which is honored in today's feast.

When you meditate on My crucifixion, understand My personal call to you, My child, to allow Me to imprint My wounds upon you, indelibly impregnating those sacred marks of My own flesh into your flesh. In this time of apostasy it is becoming more and more necessary for the world to know that I am Who am, and that My Father is allowing My presence to be made known in ways not often hitherto permitted. The world must see My stigmata, not to be mourned over, but to be meditated upon and understood as centers of love united to, through, in, and with the wounds of My children. The world misunderstands the truth of wounds. They are visible centers from which the life of healing and renewal can be known and realized.

Yes, the wounds of My body are signs of My death and when they are given by My Father's permission to My children they witness also to My resurrection and glorification.

The stigmata are signs of glory, the signs of the fullness of My life on earth. When accepted by those to whom My Father gives them, they are a dramatic living witness to the fact that one does not glorify My Father without a willing acceptance of the cross, which is in His plan for the salvation of all His children. The cross which one is required to accept is the one He has planned. It has been lived out in My life for all to see and experience in the daily renewal of My crucifixion in the Sacrifice of the Mass, preserved in full view for all time.

I speak the Truth as taught by My Father when I say in Holy Scripture that there is no salvation outside the Church. This is because the Church is the Mass and the Mass is I, Jesus, in the fullness of My crucifixion, where My children are able to eat My flesh and drink My blood in order to have life everlasting. Without embracing the fullness of the cross and obeying My Father's commands, there is no salvation. You, My Father George, and your priests must know and teach this without ceasing. This is your beautiful work and task in Cor Christi Trinitatis, wherein you will live your own joyful crucifixion and experience your own glorious resurrection.

Teach Me in My Eucharistic presence to Our world, so all will know that I, the Lord, the Church, the Cross, and the Eucharist are inseparable and necessary in order to come to the Father for eternity. My priests, love with the love of the heart of the Trinity which will be witnessed now through the stigmata, seen or unseen, but always known in the hearts and hands of you who are the priests of My heart and hands. Give Me to My Father's world which must now see Me as never before. Let My Father, and only My Father, be the judge of those who accept Me and who recognize Me. Only My Father can do that. You, My priests of My heart accept as your joyful life's work the embracing of My children in all their cries and thirsting. Carried by your anointed hands, lead them into your own graced, priestly wombs to live in your anointed hearts. Touch My suffering children with your wounded and anointed hands and hearts and place their hearts into Mine at the sacramental moment of each Mass you celebrate. My heart bleeds with an unending stream of receptivity and anointing of the hearts you place into Mine at the altar when you elevate the host and say with Me, "This is My Body which will be given up for you," and as you elevate the chalice and say with Me, "This is My Blood shed for you so that sins may be forgiven."

The consecration is the moment of the great unity of Our hearts, My Father George, the moment of the great unity of the hearts of all priests, a unity of the heart of the priest of Melchizedek with the heart of the High Priest, unified in a fusion of the two hearts. This is the very moment of oneness, that new state of being where the ontological change in the being of the priest is signified and identified, to be known forever in eternity. This signification is in all My priests forever, whether they accept Our Father's will or deny it. This signification is forever. At this moment I Myself am not only with you in a fusion of hearts, My priest, but I am also open in a most precious way to receive the hearts of those suffering children whom you present to Me at the altar. I pray before My Father at that moment that they will accept His will and openly come through Me to Him. It is the principal desire of the heart of the Trinity that Our children will want to do so. Some, however, say, "No, Lord, not Your way, but mine!"

My priests, honor your hands and your heart, and honor the wounds that are placed there, to be seen or not to be seen, though always to be experienced and known. *[Editors note: These wounds may be mystical only, and not physical. Then they are experienced in faith alone.]* Honor the wounds placed on your feet as well. When you go home so exhausted in your own work of obedience to Our Father's will, as I was exhausted in Gethsemane in obedience to Him as well, and you think you cannot walk another mile for Me, meditate on the wounds of your feet as one with the wounds of My feet, and you will walk the extra mile with joy.

We love you as the priests of My heart, the heart of the Trinity. Never forget that your life is the life of the Eucharist. My Mother will never cease to carry you in her heart. She always brings you to Me. Pray daily, My priests, to Our beautiful Mother who loves you very much. Ask her to come to you at your death on earth and she will come to you and take you by her hand to Me, and I will take you home to Our Father.

I leave you now to meditate on My love, the love of the Holy Spirit, and the love of My Mother. This is the life of Wisdom, through which you will know the life and love of the Father.

I am always with you. I will teach you again, My love, so that you and your priests of Cor Christi will know Me in ways that will allow others to come to Me for all eternity in a fusion of hearts.

Amen

## 22. COR CHRISTI'S HOME

February 17, 1993
Feast of the Seven Founders of the Order of Servites
Mt. St. Mary's Grotto Chapel
Emmitsburg, Maryland

*At prayer before the Eucharist*

*I go so far from You, and You never seem to withdraw. I am so ungrateful for the gifts of pain You give to me, and yet I know the gifts are of Your love. I run and turn away from Your challenges in love to abandon myself to You, and yet You wait for my return. You allow me, again and again, to know I can do nothing that does not begin with You.*

My Father George, you do not run away from Me, you run away from yourself, placed as you are in My heart. You try to pull yourself out of My heart. I will not let you. Do not fear the intimacy of love that I am giving you. I, the Lord, am demanding much from you. At this time I am calling you in the depths of your heart to make a total and complete surrender to My heart and also to My will for you, which is My Father's will, shared through My heart with yours. Do not be so afraid to let go. You have surrendered so much of yourself, but it is not yet total.

Today you sought security in the processes of your own mind and will regarding the home for Cor Christi. My Father and I will take you to your home. Let Us show it to you. Let it be revealed through the hierarchy of the Church. Be patient. The time is near and the place is chosen. It is not yours to choose. Let Us make the presentation. You are the priests of Cor Christi. We know where Our heart lives and you will be brought to Our home which is waiting for you. Pray, my Father, pray in rest and great peace. We love you and Our seminarians very much. Peace be yours forever and ever and ever.

Amen

## 23. "LOOK INTO MY EYES"
### January 24, 1993
### Third Sunday in Ordinary Time
### Grotto Chapel
### Mt. St. Mary's Seminary
### Emmitsburg, Maryland

*In prayer before the Eucharist and the images of the Immaculate Heart of Mary and the face of Christ—praying with Cor Christi.*

Look into My eyes. Why do you look anywhere else? Only My eyes can look into your heart. Again and again I ask you to look into My eyes. You say, "Yes, Lord," but you simply stop and glance and continue your work. My dear Father George, you must listen to Me now in this recitation of the Glorious Mysteries of the rosary. You have begun this prayer of the rosary contemplating the heart of Our Mother, wishing to gain an understanding of the unity of Our bleeding hearts—and she has placed you into Mine. You came before Me then, and you responded to My request.

Today I hold you firmly before Me to look into My eyes, even for a brief moment, to teach you the next lesson in listening. You have learned to listen to Me in our personal dialogues, and there is a beautiful relationship of our hearts when I speak to you at those times. But My call to look into My eyes is to give you a direct passage into My heart so that you may hear in an even deeper way. My Father George, this hearing will be, and now must be, physical, with our hearts touching and bleeding in unity with the bleeding heart of My Mother. I speak about the "physical" aspects of listening that exist in the interior life of the mystery of the Trinity where our relationship now rests. The listening that binds you to Me must be total. Speak to your young men, and come back to Me here at this place at a later time.

Amen

*Oh Jesus, please do not cease speaking at this time. If it would please*

*You, I want to understand this more deeply.*

*After a short period of private prayer, Our Lord spoke again.*

What I am trying to teach you, My loving priest, is to come into Me with your whole soul, body, and mind as I also come into you in soul, body, and mind when you receive Me in the Eucharist. What I am telling you is something that I give to My priests of Cor Christi, and to you, as one who must teach Me in the Church. What I am teaching you has to do with the life of transfiguration and the life of glorification. It is a preordained preliminary glimpse of life as it will be without the body you carry now. I want you to know the physical transfigured oneness in Me that is not tangible, that will be yours for all eternity, and theirs who choose to come to Me.

I want you to begin to know this so you can teach My children in the world about Me in a depth that they will understand and want to live in, where they, too, can touch this mystery. The life and the oneness I speak of is most closely achieved, in the bodily life you now have, through the eyes of one another. So many poets call the eyes the doorway to the soul. Today I call them the passages to the heart. This teaching is for the priests of My heart, whom I am training through you. You already know how your hearts can ache when they do not touch one another.

When you love each other through each other's eyes and smiles, you have a prefigurement of the transformed state of transfiguration. You are experiencing the physical in a non-tangible way. When I say, "Look into My eyes," it is not in order just to see, but to enter into Me, into My interior life, from the center of your interior life. There, in that interior center, as I have already told you, is the bleeding and breathing heart anointing Us in Our physical, non-tangible unity. This unity finds its whole new transfigured form in the heart of the Trinity, where you will be one with the transformed victims of love forever. There I will be your High Priest as We forever share in the blessed vision of My Father in a oneness which is physical, yet non-tangible.

Always stay one with your men in prayer. At these times of prayer let them lead. Be their servant in love as I always have asked you to be. But in these hours bow to them even more deeply before My presence in humility, as you watch with Me their entrance into the priesthood we share.

Amen

# 24. THE MODEL OF MULTIPLE COMMUNITIES
March 1, 1993
Ferial Day
Private Residence
Sunapee, New Hampshire

*While kneeling in the dark in my bedroom in thanksgiving*

I speak of the unity of My Mother's heart and My own.

You have now begun to live the life for which you have been created from all eternity. Your work is for the fullness of My Mother's reign on earth as the Mother of My heart, which is known on earth in the Eucharist. Your days in Cor Christi are now surpassing the first phase of your formation. The second phase is a unity with others whom We have also formed. With them you will bring into being several communities formed under the banner of My bleeding and Sacred Heart. My heart has been wounded by a never ending stream of insults and calumny which has increased beyond comprehension in exponential multiplication from the very last breath I drew on the Cross until now.

The world has been driven so far away from My heart by the attacks of Satan and his cohorts, leveled first of all against those who were known to love Me and My Mother, those who stood by Me at the cross. Satan had little success for a while. But before long many people turned away from Me, taking on their shoulders the self-centered, prideful burden of the illusion that they were the source of all the knowledge necessary to carry out the world's works.

The passing on of that self-centered pride that "I am God," deeply placed in so many human hearts, is the "Great Disfunctionality." It has been passed on through thousands of years of families genealogical histories, reaching its climax in this century, a time that witnesses to, and exhibits, the proud victories of Satan over many souls. In this time of Satan's attempts to conquer the earth, it is again necessary for My heart to suffer a second martyrdom in the world, chosen now because of My Father's great love for His creation. This martyrdom will be experienced in My priestly heart in the priests of Cor

Christi. They are being formed as those hearts who have accepted in love My call to live as co-redeemers, in its full meaning, with My Mother, for the salvation of the earth. You will be the priests to go forth and die with My own heart fused into yours, as you complete on earth that which I, Jesus the Christ, did not complete in My suffering (Col. 1:24), a most necessary sacrifice to be lived out at this time of the second Advent. As victim priests you will be the witnesses to the Light that the world will see once again. For the world will see the unity of hearts, My heart with My Mother's in yours. Then, as priests of Cor Christi, you will be the very torchbearers on earth in whom the unity of Our hearts will be seen clearly and visibly.

Your lives will be lived out in the model of My crucifixion, again unified in a most intimate way with Mary and John, as at the first crucifixion. The model never changes: My Father present in the world through Jesus the Christ through My Mother Mary.

The communities of Cor Christi have now been made evident to you so you can see and understand their relationships. There will be multiple communities: My priests as My heart, My vowed daughters as My Mother living in My heart, and the laity as the Royal Priesthood. As in the first Advent, so now in the second, My priests will find their consolation and healing love in My Mother living in her vowed daughters. As My Mother led Me to persevere in carrying out My Father's will, so too, now My Mother will live in and with the sisters, My daughters of Cor Christi, who, by their contemplative lives, will be your house of prayer. My Mother will live in these women to keep you, the priests, under her mantle as you persevere in carrying out My Father's will. In this same way she lived for Me, especially during My Passion, which will now be experienced by all of you according to My Father's plan.

You will know the great beauty of the Passion before you know its great pain. John is with you to love you, and with Mary to live in a special way with the sisters of Cor Christi Eucharistia. The sisters are not My heart, as are the priests, but they will live in My heart, as Mary does. It is where all women are meant to live and love. Many do not love any more because they no longer live in My heart. The Cor Christi family will live the model of My Father's plan for life in the world, completed by the charism of the laity to be Cor Christi Regale Sacerdotium, *the Royal Priesthood of My heart*, building Gens Sancta, *the Holy Nation*.

These graces to renew the world one more time in this model will not come to earth again. This is Our only plan. You will now rest, My Father George, as I mentioned to you when I visited with you last, for you now know the whole pattern of the Cor Christi communities. You will build these communities which will reach out to God and earth simultaneously on a great cross of hospitality, alive and on fire with the love of My heart.

These outstretched arms are truly now the arms of all the members of your own Cor Christi family: priests, religious, and laity. These arms will slowly and steadily move forward in a grand embrace of divine love, bringing all My Father's children of every race and creed, who know Me in so many ways, into My heart in the Eucharist. There they will all see Me as I am, I, Jesus, Who was sent by My Father to be crucified in love for the unity of their hearts with My heart and Our Mother's heart so that all hearts may live in the heart of the Trinity.

Now My heart is to be given form in Cor Christi. As you love, all will be able to see that I am the One who is living the life of love in you, and that I have died for all. This manifestation of My heart will not be repeated. Rest in the great peace of My heart, My beautiful sons and daughters of Cor Christi.

Good night. All of you who are to be in this work are held in Our hearts, your spiritual home.

Amen

## 25. ST. JOSEPH
March 19, 1993
Feast of St. Joseph
Private Residence
Bursin par Burtigny, Switzerland

*The dialogue began during a mid-morning prayer at home and contin-*
*ued after a meditation before the Eucharist in church in the nearby*
*town of Rolle, where I often go for Mass and meditation.*

*Lord, I hear You nearby. Where are You, Lord? In my heart and in*
*my pain I know You. So much of the world does not know You and*
*seems to be against You. Do these people to whom I am speaking even*
*care, Lord?*

Trust, trust. The world is filled today with so much confusion, and
you are being surrounded by it in these days of the formation in
your work. It will seem to you that your efforts have no purpose.
There are many spirits working against you to discourage you. They
are trying to make you walk away. Your greatest pain will be caused
by those in the Church who will deny Me, as My apostle Peter denied
Me. This denial will be in a different form. It will not always be total,
but will often take the form of changing your story. Some people will
decide that what you are saying is not really true.

When you tell the story of your work with its origin in Calcutta
and Manila, this will be as when on earth I told the story of My life
with its origin in the Father. This will sometimes be a cause of jealousy among your peers who are in the priesthood: in the Royal Priesthood and in the privileged Priesthood of Melchizedek, who were ordained to suffer and die for Me at this time of history.

You have realized that by dying for Me you are making an offering of love which is itself a gift from My Father. It is the greatest gift
We can give to one of Our children: the crucifixion of My life placed
into your life. My Father and I are with you at every moment of your
pain, especially when you are calumniated by your own colleagues in
the priesthood who serve with you at My altar of great love. Jealousy
is often in their hearts. Give Me your pain and those who work against

the success of Our work, the success of Cor Christi Trinitatis.

Teach people to pray. Teach this to the leaders who will be given to you. This is the key to your work of bringing your love for the Eucharist into the world. Leaders must come to see Me as I am: living with them in the Eucharist. They must realize that the Eucharist is I, the Lord, present and one with them. This can happen. The road of life is difficult for those who do not know Me in the Eucharist.

You, Father George, and your men who will follow you, must live according to the model you have come to know in the Trappist monks with whom you have lived for so many years in a beautiful unity of hearts. In My Father's plan I have given you to each other, as they too realize. The monastery of these men called the Strict Observance is the home of My heart, and so also shall be Cor Christi Trinitatis: Cor Christi Sacerdotes, *the ordained priests*, Cor Christi Eucharistia, *the vowed sisters*, and Cor Christi Sacerdotes Regale, *the royal priests, the laity.*

You will all answer My call to obey in love. Your work is to teach others to do this also. You must do it in love. Live together to prepare to be teachers of My Eucharistic presence in the world. You must all be masters of the life of prayer and masters in teaching others to pray, especially those who are called to be active in the affairs of the world. If you are to build the Holy Nation in accordance with My Father's will, you must realize that it can only be accomplished if I am working with you as well, guiding all the efforts of each person. Those who are building the Holy Nation can only learn how to do this through prayer where they will hear Me through whatever ways My Father chooses to employ. The goal is dual: both to know Me and to hear Me in the Eucharist.

**The New World Order is of man who wishes to be as God, whereas the Holy Nation is a world of order lived in the love of God. The first is a road to death. The second is a life of eternal holiness and love. Cor Christi members are to be the "Bilderbergers" of the Holy Nation.** You must form the hearts of these leaders, orienting them in a new direction and turning them to Me so that they will experience a daily conversion to Me through the unity of our hearts in love. This is the goal of the charism of all the branches of Cor Christi. You are being asked to do this now. My heart, held in My Mother's heart, is guiding you. You will share every pain and joy each of Us has ever known. God's will shall be done on earth as it is in heaven.

Your members must have, and will have, an undivided heart and single-mindedness of conviction in response to this call. If any sort of duality exists that would permit other goals to appear and be prolonged for more than a short period, the persons involved should realize that they are being tempted by Satan, acting as an angel of light. They are to come to Me in prayer. Let them make their choice for this work or for another! If any duality remains in their hearts after a serious time of prayer before the Eucharist, Cor Christi must dismiss them from every category of this work or they will be a source of great division. **Cor Christi cannot be divided.** Your work will be filled with mistakes, and many imperfections of its members will be evident, but these will never divide you. These imperfections become crosses and sources of love between your hearts and Mine, and the heart of Our Mother, who will give you the grace to love each other all the more.

To try to follow or to direct one's life by two or more principal goals will only result in confusion and self-destruction; such an attempt is due to a deception by Satan. You cannot work for two masters. The only multiplicity of goals that can be allowed are those that are within the total charism of the multiple communities of Cor Christi. This charism has been given to you again today in a very clear way on this great feast of St. Joseph, the husband of Mary and the foster father of Me, the Lord.

Let St. Joseph be your personal protector together with Saint John the Evangelist. St. Joseph must now be a part of the Cor Christi life for I see clearly that your stability as a community will often be undermined. Satan knows this to be your Achilles heel, and he will try to destroy you, principally through your tendencies to be unsure and afraid and to doubt what you are being called to do. Be aware that I also know this. When lack of stability happens, embrace Joseph. He will defend you in very powerful ways against Satan. He lived to de-

fend My own family. I give him to you to defend your family. He has
asked Me to let him live with you, as John also did. Never leave their
sides. Joseph will defend you in attacks against stability. John will
protect you in your life in the Church, holding you always before the
Immaculate Heart of Our Mother, who will dispense all the graces
you will need for this work of My own heart, Cor Christi.

The task of Cor Christi is nearly impossible from almost every
point of view, but if those who are the top leaders of the world will
open their hearts to My presence, I will enter their hearts and redi-
rect all they are doing to My Father's love. You will be men and women
of sacrifice and prayer to such an extent that you will know how to
address the devastation in today's world, for in your fasting and praying I will be present in your hearts, together with My Father and the
Spirit. We will guide you so that you will know what We wish to be
done in Our world.

You are to be teachers in the market place, in the streets of the
rich, who are My poorest poor, and in your seminaries and retreat
centers. Be the men and women of strict observance out in the world
as well as at home. The Cistercian monks descended from La Trappe
are your place of refuge where your heart will find My heart in the
hearts of My Trappists. They will be your model showing you how to
hold on to, and to live, the hermit's heart in love.

You will all come under attack, and in many unimagined ways.
As the work succeeds you will have a sufficient share of My crucifixion to protect you. Pray about this in the prayer life of the community and pray for this work. Your sharing in My crucifixion must be
known so well that it will become as intimate as your own breathing.
You will come to know ever more deeply your oneness with My bleeding heart, through which your whole being will become anointed as
you rest in Me in My womb. I will take you into the womb of the
Trinity. In a certain way you are conceived in, and proceed from, the
womb of My Mother, who holds us all in her great love, sharing it
with all of us in her special way. This way can be recognized by the
rays of love that pour forth from her heart and her womb, as she lives
and loves with us in the mutual breathing and beating of our hearts.

Place your head on My chest now, My dear Father George, and let Me hold it next to My heart. Teach all the men and women of Cor Christi to do likewise, and teach the world to do the same. That is My call to you, and it will never change. You all live in Our love.

*There was a period of silence and personal prayer during which I shared my deepest needs and petitions for strength and guidance. He spoke again.*

Misunderstanding is the source of the greatest pain one can know. I lived a life that was totally misunderstood, and yet by it the world was redeemed. You in Cor Christi will be living your entire lives as co-redeemers with My Mother as your model and guide, so it is necessary that you be misunderstood. That is the criterion for being co-redeemers and children of the Trinity. Not all the world knows Me even now, and many fewer know My Mother. Many misunderstand who she is in My Father's plan.

The time is upon us now to begin this work for the world is breaking as it has never broken before. Many who have never listened to Our call will now show interest in it through the call of Cor Christi. You yourself have experienced so many examples of this throughout the world: in the Philippines, Italy, France, Switzerland, England, North Ireland, and the Republic of Ireland, Canada, Argentina, and the United States.

Your encounters will not always be easy, but they will be worth the suffering that they bring to you, for every encounter will be given by My Father and by Me. We have shown you this, Father George, as now in Switzerland a group of people whom I love, are not recognizing My presence and the presence of My Mother as we wish them to do. They have probed you without ceasing, both on this visit and on your last visit, asking: What is the nature of your work? Though they do not comprehend it yet, they have indicated by their words that they recognize the work of the Catholic Church, and of the Holy Father in particular, to be a great source of stability in the world. They are interested in the work of Cor Christi for they see in it something of the Pope's stability, and perhaps even of truth. It is important for all of you in Cor Christi to recognize this.

Know, Father George, that your pain is My pain and that it unifies our hearts and allows them to pour forth a great love in the blood of the Lamb. It is the love the world must come to see and to know.

Be peace, be love, and be for Me.

Amen

# 26. LIFE, UNITY, EUCHARIST
April 4, 1993
Palm Sunday Vigil
St. Clement of Rome Catholic Church
Metairie, Louisiana

*Eucharistic Adoration, Evening Prayer, Antiphon Psalm 119:*
"Day after day I sat teaching you in the temple and you did not lay hands on me. Now you come to scourge me and lead me to the cross."

I have given you this trial at the beginning of Holy Week so that you may come to know My suffering, caused by the invasion of Satan into all of My Father's plans. You are accepting the suffering you are experiencing in the manner that I have been teaching you for a very long time. Accept it in obedience as My Father's will, and give it back to Him through Me, your Lord. Last Holy Thursday you suffered the calumniation of the Catholic Church by a Protestant Naval Chaplain. You accepted his criticism in great pain and turned it over to the Father through Me. On this eve of Palm Sunday My Father has given you a special opportunity to be a victim priest for His Church. You must expect to suffer in increasingly painful ways during every Holy Week, My Father George, for you must know the fullness and depth of all the pain and suffering that I had to experience as the time approached for My presence in the Eucharist.

That same pain must be experienced by any priest who commits himself to carry My Eucharistic presence into the world. Your life and your work are fused into an inseparable unity with My Body and Blood in the Eucharist. Cor Christi is committed by its way of life to make the Eucharist known and loved throughout the world. Satan hates you and your work, My priest of the Eucharist, and has begun to bring doubt into the minds of your seminarians. He is trying to confuse them and is tempting them to believe that there is a division between you and their Father Superior. There is not. Pray for these men, so good, so young, and so new to seminary life, so that they will see what is happening with My Father's permission and in His Providence. The opportunity to resolve this misunderstanding will be given them when they witness the great love between you and their Father Superior during your visit in May, the month of My Mother. She holds them all in her heart and in her arms.

You will suffer much, My priest, in ways only you will know, as you and your work will be subject to many diverse attacks. Satan does not want your work to succeed but it is already succeeding because My Father and I are guiding it. Be willing, My Father George, to take into your heart and body whatever you will be asked to suffer for the work's fruition. Your suffering is of the Eucharist, which is of My own death and resurrection. So, too, you must know all the pain that is required of one who is to be a priest of the Eucharistic renewal of the world. My Father's will shall be done. Pray and pray and come directly to Me at every moment of every attack as you did tonight. I will be, and want to be, one with you in these periods of suffering. In Me and through Me you will discover the full meaning of My life in yours, the meaning of My crucifixion. You have received with great grace this latest challenge to suffer. You must always do so in this way, for this suffering is, in fact, only the beginning. My Mother and I are with you, My priest. Rest in Our hearts now and into eternity.

Amen

## 27. MEDJUGORJE – GOOD FRIDAY
April 9, 1993  9 A.M. to 12:15 P.M.
Good Friday
Cross Mountain, Medjugorje
Bosnia-Hercegovina

*Praying on the Way of the Cross, I was asking the Lord to help me understand the confusion that has gripped three of the seminarians in our Cor Christi group. I began my prayer at the beginning of the stations.*

The seminarians have been placed in a situation which affords them the opportunity to learn that healing comes from overcoming division and that there is no need for a split. They are caught up in the American solution, "do it my way," without much consultation!

*I also meditated on Father Svet's words to me: Everyday is a death, a martyrdom. We become broken, alive for Christ, or dead by turning away from Him.*

*II Station. Jesus carries His cross.*

Never stop loving. Consider some way of beginning formation before your candidates enter a seminary.[1]

*IV Station. Jesus meets His mother.*

Father George, they are listening to too many voices. My Cor Christi charism is communicated by only one voice. Some of them listen to so many viewpoints that they are missing the call which is simple and direct and which is getting lost in so many voices. The message of

---

1. Cor Christi has established a basic fomation for those in all states of life consisting in attendance at its principal monthly meetings in their region for one year before applying to be an Associate Member.

Cor Christi must always be presented with great clarity. Father Svet grasps it clearly. Talk with him about division in communities.

Do not let fear have a place in Cor Christi. There is fear now in the hearts of a few, which confuses their thinking. They gather too many opinions and try to make them consistent with each other. All the opinions they hear are well-meant, but they are not in agreement. They often come from good people with different understandings of Cor Christi. These people give their best answers, but not one of them has the charism I have given to you. They listen to you, but not all of them hear you, because their hearing is not open to the charism as you are giving it to them. That is because they are prejudging what you are telling them according to the interpretations of others, whose understanding of the charism is partial.

You must gather them and teach them and at the same time listen to their questions. Their observations are truly their observations and are given in love. Accept their corrections when they apply. You will know when that happens. Pray.

*Time in silent prayer before Station IV. Then Jesus continued:*

Be for them a mother's womb in all your maleness. This share in My cross is your gift this Good Friday. I have been teaching you to value this sharing in different ways all week, even in your respiratory problems, which have increased as the pains in your hands have decreased. It is all part of your acceptance to be a victim priest. Offer all of your suffering for My priests who are lost and broken. Cor Christi will be under great attack from within and from without and will be broken for Me, alive, which is the only way that is redemptive. Follow prayerfully the counsel Father Svet gave you. *[Father Svet said that all persons broken in life are then alive for Christ or dead by turning against Him.]*

You are My instrument to teach the seminarians the cross. You are not special, but what I have been teaching through you is special. The reality of the crucifixion holds their attention. My children have forgotten it and think of it as an idea. Now, for the first time, they are realizing that they are being asked to live it. That is critical for them to see. They must understand that it is part of their vocation, not separate from it. Yes, through crucifixion the call to undivided love is confirmed and unified in a charism given by My heart and placed in each individual's heart. At this time, they are trying to discern whether it is really necessary to carry the cross. I have given this charism of the cross not only to Cor Christi but to the Church.

The charisms given to Cor Christi are true, explicit, and in My Father's plan. Cor Christi will succeed in accordance with Our plan, but you must be aware of two main issues: 1) the current confusion results from too many simultaneous sources of information and 2) the Cor Christi charism must be given clearly to them, even if one member has said he cannot handle any more right now. He must.

*VI Station. Veronica wipes the face of Jesus.*

Keep an open heart to receive help, always. Never judge. Purgatory, as you saw when My Mother showed it to you, is filled with people who never fulfilled their share in living the crucifixion which My Father and I gave them. Let the seminarians wrestle but keep them focused on the charism, even if they reject it. It may add to their suffering but to make a choice they must see those dialogues that apply. They must embrace the privilege of the cross to avoid purgatory. This is always the first choice of Jesus, the Lord, and of My Father.

*I pray that I may appreciate the care the seminarians try to give and do give to me, Lord, and I am grateful. I hope and pray they spend time on themselves as well.*

*I spoke to Jesus about the cultural problems in America that hinder people from living the cross.*

To live in Cor Christi is totally un-American for it demands resignation to an obedience from without, one that the person cannot manipulate nor maneuver to fit his or her own decisions. Even in the spiritual life, Americans will take the spiritual gifts I give and shape them into a comfortable agreement with what I have given them as material gifts. The material method and the spiritual method of responding to challenges are very different. The American approach to the solution of spiritual problems is to apply material methods.

Pray for America. It is in deep spiritual trouble and has become a land of legalized death. Pray, pray, pray for America. Everyone who comes to Cor Christi from America will be filled with American ways. These will often have to be changed if the person is to acclimatize himself or herself to the Cor Christi way of life. America looks to self. Cor Christi must look to the Father and to eternity!

Amen

## 28. THE MASS
May 11, 1993
Vigil of St. Pancras
Private Residence
Ellicott City, Maryland

*In prayer in my room before celebrating Mass for the Tuesday night Marian Prayer Group*

The Mass is the Great Prayer, the ongoing life of the redemptive and salvific reality of the death and resurrection of the Lord.

Through My Father's gift of the Mass, redemption and salvation take place on earth daily. It is a gift given in order that the world may never be separated from its necessary connection to the transfigured world of glory where all persons live in an unending existence with the fullness of the life of the Trinity.

The sacrifice of the Mass is the primary model of life as it is to be lived on earth. In the Mass, the worlds of heaven and earth are united. It is the world's primary event, the sacred moment of unity wherein the unification of creation with the Creator will always be able to take place.

The Mass is the only place since Calvary where My presence is full and complete on earth for all time. At Calvary I drew all of mankind into My heart and placed it into the heart of My Father.

I gave the Mass to the world so that through My sacrifice the human family would always be united. It is ordained to bring all those to My Father who place their hearts into My heart at the moment of consecration. At this moment My blood is shed sacramentally as My crucified Self is present daily on earth. The Mass is where the crucified hearts of My Mother and Myself are united with My Father's children in a bleeding that anoints them with a deep understanding that one must die in order to live and rise into a life that is eternal. The Mass is the locus for life's meaning on earth.

Begin to make this a central theme of your preaching.

Amen

# 29. THE IMMACULATE HEART
June 19, 1993
Feast of the Immaculate Heart of Mary
Ninth Anniversary of Ordination
Small Chapel, Pontifical Collegio Filipino
Rome, Italy

*At prayer, a holy hour, during a visit with Cardinal Sin*

You, with all of the members of this work, are to live in the heart of Mary. My Father is giving you, as a gift, the same residence that He has given to the Holy Spirit. It is your home for all eternity. To live in the Immaculate Heart of Mary is to be one with My own Heart. The priests of Cor Christi are My Heart and as such they are held in the womb of Mary's heart.

The Sisters will live in My Heart as do the laity who, related to My Heart, are at the same time held in the womb of My Mother's heart. In your Spencer retreat, Father Raphael spoke of My Mother's heart being the lining of My Heart. The intimacy of this image is very beautiful.

The oneness of hearts is directly related to their purity, as the name "Immaculate" indicates. For only in immaculate purity can there be a union of hearts. In such a union, hearts come together without agenda and with an openness of charity that wishes to, and can, receive each other.

Mary's heart lives fully in Mine. My Heart is one with the heart of My Father. You, with all the Cor Christi members, must place your hearts in My Mother's. Then she will place your hearts into Mine, where she resides, and I will place your hearts into the heart of the Trinity. I have shown this to you before. Now I want you to know that in this life of shared hearts you are fully embraced by the Holy Spirit. His life with My Mother is a nuptial life from which Wisdom proceeds. A life in union with the heart of Mary, where the Holy Spirit who overshadows Mary resides, is a life that tastes the presence of God, known interiorly in a nearly tangible way as Truth, flowing from the intimate union of Mary and the Holy Spirit. To know Wisdom is to taste the presence of God.

Cor Christi is being called into existence now to teach the Church the depth of prayer and sacrificial abandonment that is requisite for losing one's heart in Mary's heart. Once that gift of sacrificial abandonment of one's heart is made, one becomes the joyful donor of one's heart to the hearts of Jesus and Mary and to the Father, where one tastes God interiorly. That is the great gift of Wisdom. Then, and only then, can one begin to know God, the plan of salvation and redemption, and holy suffering, and come to know the cross as essential to human life,

Cor Christi has the key to renewing the life of the Church and the world by teaching, and bringing about the conversion of hearts to this way of life. This process of conversion begins and ends in abandonment to Me in the Eucharist, My real presence on earth. Thus all persons can develop a love affair of hearts—theirs with Mine.

You, Father George, are coming to know well the redemptive joy that results from a life of suffering. Therefore you can bring this knowledge to others who cry out for it. In most of the world the Church has abandoned the beautiful truth of the sacrificial life of the ordained priesthood, the truth of My presence in the Eucharist, and the truth that the laity are commanded in Scripture to live as a Royal Priesthood, building a Holy Nation. My life in the Eucharist is almost abandoned throughout the world. This is why My Father, in His great mercy and love, is exposing His heart one more time to all His children in the world, in the hope that they will see how His heart is calling out for their love with great passion, crying out to all to receive His love. The relationship with Him must be repaired to heal the Great Abortion which I have mentioned before.

Among all the beautiful works in the Church, the work of Cor Christi, centered on the Holy Sacrifice of the Mass, is one of the most important works My Father is giving to the Church at this time of her near destruction. Her wounds will be massive, which is part of My Father's plan for her purification. As I had to die in order to rise, so too, My Mystical Body on earth has to go through this near-death purification. You know the pattern well, Father George, and so do those whom we send to you.

Follow the plan given to you in My love to train all the applicants for priesthood in the Cor Christi way of life. They can be ordained for all the dioceses throughout the world and bring this Eucharistic way of life with them to all persons. These priests, while spreading this love to all who are willing to receive it, will remain in contact with the Cor Christi Institute as its members. They will form a very beautiful family of priests living the Cor Christi life according to its rule. This widespread group, the priestly order of Cor Christi, will be a special presence in the Church.

As never before the Church desperately needs a renewal of unity so that all My Father's children will experience and come to know the exquisite truth that it is only in the Eucharist, with the Eucharist, and through the Eucharist that salvation can be received and life can be lived. One who lives a redeemed life cooperates with our Father's plan. Redeemed lives build a Holy Nation. And the immaculate hearts of the priests, who are of My Mother's heart and My own, will at last shine in the world. This can only come from a genuine awareness of My Eucharistic presence.

Be My life in the Eucharist for all in My Father's world to see, that they may know My Father's plan to bring a reign of peace to the world. Renew My Church and the earth so that all will always know My true presence. You will suffer, but I will support you.

In the life of union of immaculate hearts there will be a foretaste of eternity, and a joy and love visible to all, which bespeak unity. This is something the world has never seen. A disunited priesthood participates in the Great Abortion, because it aborts God's command to love one another as He loves us.

Provide the rules for a life which brings one to experience Wisdom and to know eternity as one's real and primary goal, a goal in which hearts are bound together in unity.

Father George, in this way of life of Eucharistic oneness, the life of faith is constant and this is the source of great peace. In the lived Cor Christi life, one is always in love and knows by faith that one is secure in God, who is experienced in the overlay of hearts. Love is faith actualized. It yields the knowledge of who one is. Faith is the confirmation of the correctness of what one is doing—living in a love affair with one's God. The world needs to understand this.

This gift is being given now. You are all held in Our Hearts as you go about this privileged task of faith in the great love that you now realize you have. You have it because you have accepted and given meaning to the suffering which God has allowed you to undergo. Father George, your heart is united with the heart of My Father as never before, and the knowledge, convictions, and faith you now have you know to be yours. This will always be the pattern of the life of Cor Christi: purification and unity. Live in My blessing and love. Happy anniversary from the Hearts of the Trinity and Our Mother. You are in Our love as We hold yours for Us.

Remember, all relationships are meant for eternity. You are united in a love grounded in a faith in each other based on the understanding that, for each of you who are related in My Heart, I am there. If you find any worry or doubt when you approach each other in carrying out My Father's plans for your lives, ask your angel to precede you as you approach one another. Your angel can prepare the heart of the receiver with the understanding needed to maintain the unity which We wish you to live on earth. The angels want to do this. Maintain a deep relationship with the angels since they are My messengers sent to assist you in bringing forth Our work on earth.

Amen

## 30. REDEMPTION
July 7, 1993
Ferial Day
On an Amtrack train
Baltimore to New York

*After four hours of spiritual reading of* To the Priests, Our Lady's Beloved Sons *and the Breviary*

To understand the world and its renewal one must first understand redemption. Your redemption begins at birth and proceeds through suffering, denial of self, and abandonment to Christ, while you are held in the Immaculate Heart of My Mother. She guides you at every moment as you learn to abandon yourself to Me. The process is very slow at times and very painful. It is the process of a complete detachment from the world. As it is accomplished, you learn how to be in the world and around the things of the world without deriving your identity from them. They now have their meaning only in terms of their own identity.

The identity of the human person comes solely from Me. We require that this abandonment into the heart of the Trinity take place through a process of detachment from the world in order to eliminate the possibility of Our children finding their identity in terms of the world.

When one's identity is founded in My Father, Myself, and My Mother, overshadowed by the love of the Holy Spirit, then the person returns to his daily involvement with the world seeing all things as they exist in their own created beauty but with a neutrality of heart and of mind that does not require the world's treasures to give one an identity separate from the life of the Trinity, which alone is the total source of the meaning of the human person.

According to My Father's plan, persons are born to continue the life of the Incarnation through the Sacrament of Baptism in such a way that they are bridges between creation and Himself. Through this Sacrament the unity of My Father and creation is restored, and the baptized person enters into the privileged and loving life of redemption and salvation, which is directed toward an eternity with the Father in the Heart of the Trinity. According to the design of My Father's mercy and salvific love, the reunion of hearts, separated by the Great Abortion, begins in Baptism, whether of water, desire, or fire. The eternal mind of the Father is one of total unity. When the unity of the Father with creation was rent through the fall of the angels, His love, in its greatness, demanded a return to unity, made possible through the sacrificial life and love of His Son.

The Father, not allowing His love to be blocked from proceeding into the world, in His love, gave the world the gift of the ordained priesthood through the Pentecost visit of His Holy Spirit. He established and called His priests, as ALTER CHRISTI, to administer the life of the Sacraments in the Church. He did this in order to effect and secure His intimate relationship with His children through the ongoing presence in the world of the hearts of the Father, Son, and Mary, our Mother, surrounded by the loving presence of her Spouse, the Holy Spirit.

The overshadowing of Mary by the Spirit is nuptial. The spousal relationship of Mary and the Holy Spirit is a model for the intimate relationship between God and man in the sacramental life. Through this evident relationship of Mary and the Spirit, the human race has the model for seeing and understanding that the relationship of all persons to God our Father is meant to be a nuptial one—a life of love in a union of hearts.

The redemptive life began with the initiative of My Father in sending the Holy Spirit to overshadow Mary, who gave birth to Me that I might suffer, die, and rise. The purpose of this redemptive life is to give all persons the desire to have, and the ability to have, union with the Trinity.

Go forth, My Cor Christi children, in boldness and security. Teach everyone My Father's loving call to be one with Him for eternity, through the sacrificial and redeeming process of grace, in the Great Nuptial Mass of the Reunion of our Father and His creation.

Go teach this to all nations with a joy that can only come from your knowing the meaning of crucifixion. All of heaven goes with you in the love of the Father, Son, Spirit, and of Mary our Mother.

Celebrate the Mass.

Teach the Mass.

Live the Mass.

Be the Mass,

for the Mass is the fullness of Our Father's presence on earth through His Son. Bring the people of the world to desire a great conversion of hearts, so that they will want to unite their hearts with My Father's heart in the Sacred Sacrifice of the Mass. May all your teachings be of the Mass as the model of life. Our children will understand this as the place wherein their lives must be lived, and wherein they will want to live. They will learn a life lived according to our Father's plan, which is that their hearts rest in the heart of the Holy Sacrifice of the Mass. They will come to know the Mass as the Grand Harmony of Love.

Amen

## 31. TRANSFIGURATION. SPEAKING THE TRUTH
### Feast of the Transfiguration
### August 6, 1993
### Sunapee, New Hampshire

*I hear Your call to listen, my Lord. Thank you for coming to me on this beautiful day of Transfiguration.*

What you are about to do at this Mass is twofold. You must understand the Mass as the most profound unity of the two dimensions of the life of Jesus, your Lord, as transfigured. The transfiguration is both of the word and of the body. I want you to see and to teach the critical importance and place the spoken word has in relation to the transfiguration. You must learn that, in the same way that there is an overlay of hearts—My Father's, My Mother's, My own, and the hearts of My children—there must also take place an overlay of speaking. This is as quintessential as the overlay of hearts. For it is from the overlay of hearts and speaking that the Truth is taught. This is the most important teaching I have given you so far. I could not give this until now, because I had to present all the teachings in the prior dialogues as the ground for this one.

Transfiguration is total, absolutely total. It includes all that is corporeal and all that is of the spirit and thought. The whole person is transfigured. On earth, My physical, human presence was not yet transfigured, but all that I spoke was transfigured. The transfiguration of the human body that was to come to Me and is to come to you was already present in My speaking and also in the speaking of My Mother. For everything We said on earth came directly from, and in unity with, the speaking of our Father. That is why it was Truth and only Truth. After My Resurrection and Mary's Assumption, Our bodies were glorified. In that process of transfiguration, a true ontological change of being, we were totally re-formed in body and spirit. Our bodies became, according to the Father's Will, one in harmony with the Truth of our speaking. You must understand this completely.

On earth the lives of My children are not transfigured, but your lives hold all the potential for that. Cor Christi's work is not, definitely not, a life of "doing" in the usual worldly sense. It is the beautiful life of teaching My children how to be Truthful. By that I mean how to speak as I speak, and as My Father speaks. Speak only what is taught by My Father. See the world through the silence of your hearts and hear in the silence of your hearts two realities: 1) the lies against My Father being spoken in the world, and 2) the Truth being spoken to you in your hearts from My Father through Me.

Look always to Mary as your model, for she lived perfectly both the listening and the speaking. Then, when you see and hear, you will be able to do what I ask of you in Cor Christi. Teach those who are brought to you the singular reality of speaking My Truth, without which essential reality the world will never be able to come to Me. The key is the complete conversion of one's heart. By this I mean the unifying of one's heart with Mine so that the heart can see and listen. Then one can speak, and be Truth.

This process of unifying one's heart and mind and speaking with Mine fosters that ontological change which begins in baptism and, for the laity, will be completed when they enter heaven. It consists in living the life of Truth, which is heard and spoken in the overlay of hearts. From this overlay of hearts, which I have taught you, and which you now know is necessarily first, comes the speaking of Truth in an analagous overlay of speaking. The ontological change for My ordained priests precedes their entry into heaven. It takes place during the ordination liturgy.

My Father speaks to the world through Me, through Me to you, and you and your priests of Cor Christi, in turn will sanctify the world through your speaking. The world is filled with the private and personal opinions of Our children and that is not what My Father wants. It is not what He wants. No personal opinion about the divine Life is worth anything unless it comes directly from My Father speaking to the world through the overlay of hearts. The total transfiguration of the world begins here: first, in the overlay of hearts in love, where the person learns to dwell and to be; then in the speaking of Truth given by My Father through Me.

The speaking of the Truth cannot happen until the hearts of Our children are purified, for only persons who have purified hearts know how to listen to My Father's Truth, so that they can then speak it. Otherwise, speaking becomes a matter of intellectual games and this is where Satan enters in, making people believe in the primary importance of the intellect. Intellect is indeed a gift of My Father, but unless the gift of purity is first realized in the heart, transfigured speech cannot proceed from the intellect. *[Editor's note: The intellect can then judge of the conformity of thought and speech with the authentic teaching of the Church.]*

I spoke to you this morning about how, through a long process of painful conversion of their hearts, the laity will come to the Truth. This conversion will end only at their death and their passing over to Me. In their ongoing, developing recognition of Truth through the purification of their hearts, they will progressively speak Truth and learn how to live in the double overlay of Our Hearts and of Our speaking.

Listen carefully, for I will now show you why the priesthood must be renewed and why I ask you in Cor Christi to do it for Me. My dear Father, you must speak to all our priests of Melchizedek in your Cor Christi life. Speak to them, speak to them in great love. I have told you in earlier dialogues of the change that begins in a priest when he answers My first call to come to Me for ordination, and that a true ontological change takes place in his heart at his ordination. He becomes at that moment like Mary, who becomes his Mother for, through his ordination, his heart is completely and totally changed and converted into the total purity of the heart of his Mother Mary and the heart of Jesus, his Lord and now his Brother. The new priest stands before the throne of God with Me and his Mother as we present his heart to his Father for all eternity so he now lives, if he remains faithful, in a way that can speak only Truth throughout the world. And as the Mass is the Great Truth on earth, the priest is now able, through his ontologically changed heart, to celebrate the Holy Sacrifice of the Mass with Me for all eternity. And yet, with all this having been given to our beloved priests, they still give in to pride as Adam did. They want to be God, and they assist in the Great Abortion of man turning away from God and from the real presence of their Eucharistic Jesus. Thus, you live, Father George, in what is the New Age, a movement which teaches mankind that the source of all being comes from himself.

Cor Christi, dear children of My Heart, is given to you on this day of special grace, so that you may live as My small children of suffering and humility in order to bring transformation to the world, as you live in the hearts of Mary, your Mother, Jesus, your Lord, and God your Father. Then Our children will again hear the Truth and speak it and live it.

Let the Feast of the Transfiguration be the great feast to be lived in accordance with the rule of life of your community and the community of Youth 2000, who are the future witnesses of Our Truth. The renewal of the world is given to you and it is beginning now. The transforming of the Protestant world will begin in England in the lives of universities under the banner of Thomas More, who is your patron for that work. Let him show you the way.

The Mass is the Transfiguration on earth. The overlay of hearts and of speaking bring the cross of conversion into your lives and bring alive in you the process of your transfiguration. This transfiguration began in Our call to you in Baptism and will be completed by your death in grace and Truth. Hence you will all stand before the Father with hearts united for eternity. There will be one voice, the voice of all creation united in glorifying God. Prepare Our world for this in ways We will show you.

Amen

## 32. A NEW ONENESS
## THROUGH A DEVOTION SPECIFIC TO COR CHRISTI
September 27, 1993
Feast of Saint Vincent de Paul
Boston, Massachusetts

I am going to speak to you tonight in a way that you have not heard before.

Amen

September 27-28, 1993
Feast of St. Vincent de Paul
11:55 p.m. - 1:00 a.m.
Following celebration of Mass
Sunapee, New Hampshire

*Oh Lord, my Jesus, tell me what you began to say at Mass. How are we to live the Mass as Cor Christi?*

The daily life of members of Cor Christi will find its center in and through the daily celebration of the separation of My Body and My Blood on the altar. The graces of this celebration will be transmitted to all members of the community through the priest celebrant, ordained to be My Heart at the very altar where I place My heart crucified through My beloved priest.

I am now able to tell you that the priests I bring to Cor Christi are to be contemplatives. They will also evangelize, going out from a community with its own monastic style. You have always known and said, since you were a child, that you would end your life as a monk. I am now allowed to disclose to you that knowledge, a knowledge held for all time in My Father's heart and passed on now through My heart to yours. My priest, listen very carefully as I speak slowly and explain to you, with powerful and simple clarity, why you must be contemplatives. The necessary center of all Cor Christi lives is the overlay of hearts, the overlay of speaking truth, and also the overlay of bodies.

This message comes to you on the feast of St. Vincent de Paul, the day that marks the beginning of your own passage into a life of total oneness in and through Me. As I bring you into this new oneness you will also realize and know, as you have not known before, how I can come into you to live through you. You are now being invited, My priest of the sacrificial life of the altar, to live in a total union with Me and thus it is necessary to live in an overlay and total unity of body, in a total life of bleeding with Me. Your body must of necessity be as Mine. The only way in which I can bring you into this total identity is through the depths of contemplative prayer. Priests of the Cor Christi Institute will be known for a while as Associates, belonging to their dioceses, as Cardinal Sin indicated, to renew the Church at large. But they cannot be Associates without a contemplative life in always increasing degrees. They will begin in the dioceses as active priests of renewal but after a number of years, perhaps five, they will return to the monastery as the core priests to live the life of total oneness of My body with theirs. Let Me explain this life in detail.

Your principal contemplation will be the one I gave you in tonight's Mass when I spoke to you at the opening prayer as you read, "God, you gave Vincent de Paul the courage and holiness of an apostle for the well-being of the poor and the formation of the clergy," and at the consecration when in your heart you heard My direction to you, which was also meant for all the priests to come.

The principal prayer of the meditation hour of the core priests will be the celebration of a private Mass of Devotion, each of you separately, during a chosen hour in the very early morning starting between 2:30 and 3:00 A.M. You are being asked to begin that hour with Mass in a private chapel with a large crucifix behind the altar. At the consecration, meditate on My physical death on the Cross. In your mind's eye look at Me in the pangs of death. Then, standing before Me, with your eyes closed and your mind and heart open, turn around and back up until you feel My last breathing and, with your hands outstretched, feel, on the back of your hands, the warm wounds on the palms of My hands being impressed on yours. Feel the wound of My Heart beat through your left side until your own heart breaks, and let your right side share the wound and the blood and water that flowed from Me. Walk in the wounds of My feet to wherever My Father and I will take you.

This meditation, My dear Father, is the wish of My Father. It is given to Cor Christi through Me as the specific prayer that will identify the core priests of Cor Christi for all eternity. You will all be known by the wounds of My Body in your bodies, however they will be realized. Each core priest's heart will be a monastic enclosure in which the Eucharistic Jesus will dwell.

Your meditation hour must be totally quiet with Mass celebrated singly or with a concelebrant and may be attended by seminarians, in complete silence. All the seminarians will share this hour of prayer in the darkness of the chapel of whatever Mass they are assigned to attend. The seminarians will serve the priests. The day will come when they too will teach others through their celebration of Mass. The seminarians must know that this hour of the morning is essential to the Cor Christi clerical life.

This period of prayer, assigned by My Father's will, is your principal hour for teaching your own. There they will learn the true meaning of evangelization: the silent witness of the union of one's heart, mind, body, and blood with Mine, which is to be taught to the world. This and only this constitutes the true life of Eucharistic Evangelization. This is how one becomes "Eucharistic," a term which I have employed many times, but have never before explained. The priests must teach this Eucharistic devotion to the royal priests of the laity who belong to Cor Christi.

In Cor Christi Eucharistia, the sisters will also arise, and a priest will celebrate an early Mass for them in their chapel in darkness.

During these morning hours you will bring *no spiritual reading, no Scripture, and no rosaries. Just your hearts and minds with no agenda.* For your community the Mass holds **first place.** During the previous evening, before bed-time, the members of the core community will review in prayer the readings for the next morning's silent Mass and time of prayer. They may make notations with pad and pencil about the readings, but may not bring the notes to Mass. The enlightenment that the priests, sisters, and candidates may receive will be transmitted at the Eucharist. The laity are not to be required to make this early morning prayer hour unless they freely choose to do so. The spiritual directors of the community must be very sensitive to the needs of the laity, who will often have obligations of family and work that require a complete night's rest.

Teach Cor Christi to be My Cross, to be My Crucifixion, to live My wounds, to live the pain of My death, including the great oppression and confusion of My mental anguish. And teach the life of Resurrection joy. Teach all of My children that salvation comes from accepting My Father's will and His plan which is set out in Scripture. Your principal Scripture for meditation, as a community, will always be the Gospel of John. It is the Gospel of the Eucharist which leads to a glorified life in eternity. It is the Gospel of the unity of earth and eternity, revealing how Our children on earth are united with the life of eternity in heaven. It is also the Gospel of beauty, the special beauty of My Passion and Resurrection as told by John, My tender and beautiful John, whom I have already given to you out of all the apostles as your principal teacher. He is ever available to all of you. He will be present to each one of you in your early morning Masses and meditations, as will be your angels. Mary and Joseph will stand beside you and beg graces from heaven for you in a special way at these times of prayer. Father George, you are answering My call to you to pray more. I had to wait for your response, which was a firm "fiat," in order to bring you this message tonight.

Cor Christi will live in the Church with great strength for it is My Father's will. You are now given the source of that strength. You will never live alone for all of heaven is with you, and We love you in ways that only heaven can.

Rest now in peace. Begin this new life slowly until you find the pattern which allows it to flow. All these night Masses must be silent.

Good night, My love. Thank you for embracing Our request to serve your poor of affluence and to be the priests and apostles We are asking you to be. This model of life is absolutely required to do the work We will give you.          Amen

# 33. THE JOY OF SUFFERING
### October 26, 1993, Tuesday
### Ferial Day
### Fatima, Portugal

*Yesterday, during the Stations of the Cross, at the second station, I understood clearly that my Father was asking me to reach out to the world's youth and to gather them into Cor Christi through Youth 2000's gift and charism. I then became aware of the nearly tangible presence of John Bosco, my patron, on whose feast I was born. I have always loved youth, and when I was young I thought I was called to gather and take care of them, but in a way that differed from John Bosco's. I did not feel called to found orphanages or schools. Later in life I encountered the souls of the young through my call to university teaching.*

*This Via Crucis today was filled with the call to suffer very much for Jesus as a victim soul—a call as essential for my own salvation as for the salvation of souls. Today's message was given to me at Fatima at the end of the same station of the Via Crucis at which I received a message on the anniversary of Mary's apparition on May 13, 1992. O Lord, thank you for the graces you bestow on my poor soul when I am in your Mother's womb in Fatima.*

*I prayed about these things that night in the Eucharistic Chapel in the Hotel Verbo Divino.*

Father George, your suffering is necessary for your life on earth as planned by My Father. You have experienced today, in a way you have not experienced before, the great desire to suffer, and the great joy that comes from the broken and bleeding heart We have given you. You felt and saw, with a deep interior vision, the presence of My bleeding Heart in front of yours. You saw your heart united to Mine. This allows you to want, for the first time, as a necessary element in your life, unity with the suffering and bleeding Heart of Me, Jesus, your Lord, with yourself.

The joy you experienced was subtle but powerful, subtle because it was felt in a deep interior silence which has given you a new stability and security unknown before today. This great and necessary suffering brings about the unity of our hearts, Mine with yours and yours with Mine. You have often spoken about and taught this to others, but now, during these few hours, I chose to gift you with a more profound understanding of this as you prayed the Via Crucis in My Mother's heart, a prayer which was uttered in turn by her Immaculate Heart.

My dear Father George, she wants you to live intimately within her heart in the depths of her womb, which is the center of the Church, so that you will be able to call out to the youth of Our world to come and live in that very same womb. You will be able to do this now, for I have allowed you to see the immense joy in suffering that exists in the center of My heart. You have come to know not only the meaning of suffering, and that it is a joyful necessity for oneness with Me, but also that you never want to be without such suffering, **for without it you would lose Me.** You have also understood that this loss is not a unique possibility for you alone, for it is a truth that applies to everyone.

Go to my youth as you go so well to the affluent poor. You have learned to bring meaning to the suffering of the affluent, who have recognized their need for conversion. Do not abandon this work of My Heart, but now go also to today's suffering youth, who find life in an affluent society without meaning. Do not concern yourself with how to do it. Once again, as in the first days of this work when you found yourself in St. Peter's Square not knowing where to begin, just begin.

My Mother and I are there beside you, one on each side. The Youth 2000 movement can guide you. Study its charism for youth, for My Mother has given it direction for this, as she gave you direction for the renewal of the leadership through My Eucharistic heart, which is My presence in the world. At the time of that call you were praying for discernment and you were given the call. You were truly called to go to leaders but the plan was always meant to unfold to this point.

Your work is to go not only to the leaders who are in power—this will always be a principal part of the charism—but also to what you now know will be the greater part, not in importance, but in number: the youth of the world who will be the next leaders. They are without meaning in every country of the world, for the poverty of affluence has caused a starvation in their souls. They have received no spiritual food and their spirit is paralyzed, locked within by feelings of abandonment and meaninglessness.

I speak these words in this manner for your encouragement; the young are not dead in spirit, but they are paralyzed to the point of not being able to hear Me or the Holy Spirit. As I have said with regard to your gift of recognizing future priests, the same vulnerability that the priest candidates see in you, the youth of all countries will see, and they will see as well that this vulnerability exists in themselves. D. has already seen it and wants to know how to attain the security he sees in you, for he knows it was not arrived at easily. Yet besides wanting it, he needs to trust in someone who can show him the way.

The young who suffer much are saying to themselves that they would willingly suffer even more, if meaning could be given to their lives of suffering without meaning. Know, My Father George, My son, My priest, that all your suffering has been for salvation, your own and others. Embrace it and share it with the world of which you have seen so much. Your colleagues of the poverty of affluence, who are converting in such numbers, will be your co-trainers and co-teachers of the young. That is why we have called both groups to you, so that each of them can experience the loving service of their broken hearts.

Bring Me to the broken hearts of the young of My Father's world. Peter is the first one called to place his broken heart, near despair, into the heart of Jesus the Lord, the High Priest, so that he may become a priest of Melchizedek for the continuation of this work. He, too, knows the meaning of the broken heart as the locus where suffering is nourished by My love, which is given to his heart, broken at such a young age. This awareness that their broken hearts are nourished by my love is given to some so that these broken hearts of My Father's youthful children can be healed and guided by men and women who have lived through the process. From a life of near despair, they, too, came to their knees as they abandoned themselves to the warmth of the united hearts and wounds of Myself, Jesus, and Mary, knowing us as Mother and Son.

They are able to share their broken hearts renewed in a love that will never die again, in a work that will endure, because it resides in the womb of the Church. I will speak to you about this in greater depth and with further directions.

Go now in peace and in My love. Live in the exchange of hearts of all those we call to work with you. Only those we call can accomplish this task. You will recognize them and know them.

Thank you for coming to pray at this precious hour of the night. Be before the Eucharist at night for a union in great love. You will hear what I want. You will know that you are to teach what I give to you. You need no other source of knowledge.

Good night. Rest in Our love.

Amen

# 34. ABANDONMENT
January 13, 1994
Feast of St. Hilary
Chapel of the Franciscan Sisters of Syracuse
Rome, Italy

Abandonment takes place in certain stages until one is separated from one's attachments. At first it is as if one's very heart is being torn out. Then one suddenly finds that the wound which was formed by the continual tearing that occurs with every letting go, with every little surrender to Me, is healed and repaired by the glorious intrusion of My Sacred Heart. One's wounded heart, after endless agonies of letting go, has finally come to Me with no agenda.

This is where I find you now, My dear Father George. You have let Me in as I have taken you in, coming to Me over so many years of surrendering to the love of the cross. You have given Me your multiple crosses in an ever increasing trust that I would carry you forever on My own Cross—which I lived out for you so that one day you would give Me all of your own crosses as I gave you Mine.

My Cross is the joyful center of human life. Life became joyful when you understood that I was delivering you from your agony through your progressive abandonment in faith—the agony of trying to find some meaning in life that would make it bearable, if not entirely worthwhile. You became aware that I, too, lived on earth on a cross. Not until you let Me take yours onto Mine did you discover that meaning in life comes only from living in and on the Cross of Jesus, your Lord, which is a great Cross of love. The crosses designed by My children are never the fruit of real love, for they are fashioned by turning to self as the source of the meaning of their lives. This is the situation of your contemporary world.

You are now ready, personally, to bring Me into this world of great self-centeredness in ways that will let My priesthood shine out. You have come through so much suffering to let Me live in you as never before. Come only to Me for all meaning, and never to any other source. All of your work will now flourish without major obstacles, for you have learned to rely on the Trinity alone to give meaning to it. I, Jesus, gave you your work in the priesthood of Melchizedek. It is never possible to comprehend its full meaning and importance by listening to anyone other than Myself or those gifted with the priesthood of the altar. Peter is one of those persons, and the one to live with you in a depth that is given from the life of the Trinity. For he, too, in his own level of acceptance and abandonment, is surrendering to Me his self-chosen crosses, and will arrive at the fullness of abandonment in the priesthood of Melchizedek.

All priest candidates, once they say "Yes," share in the priesthood, because in that first "Yes" their ontological change begins to take place. It is necessary to realize this in order to be able to recognize the persons who can understand this work. The laity will understand the work of Cor Christi only when it is taught to them by priests. No lay person can advise you on the core of the work.

This work comes from the High Priesthood to the ordained priesthood. From there it reaches the laity, whence they come to know the meaning of their Royal Priesthood, which is needed for building a Holy Nation. No matter how holy lay persons may be, they are by necessity unable to teach you what the charism is, or how it will be recognized. It can never work that way, and do not ever allow it to be attempted. My Father in heaven has allowed you to fall into the path of very holy lay persons in this last year. They can be beneficiaries of the work of Cor Christi in many ways and at many levels. But they began to direct you in the work, and you became confused by their many voices. A great weakness in your character resulting from Original Sin, is to be polite to the extent of not being able to resist the advice given to you. This occurs especially when you recognize that the advice, especially when given by women, is given in good faith and out of love,

You always weaken in the face of a woman's advice because of the great love you have for Mary, to whom you listen without reservation. You expect all women to be her representatives, especially if they are her children and possess great holiness. The only exception to this directive is Our child, Mother Teresa, who shares much of the charism given to you through her by the Trinity. This charism is now placed in your priestly life to build the leadership of the world into a renewed and holy childhood. Mother is the only woman who can advise you on your spiritual life. The rest now lies with the Trappists.

Through many events you came to know the beautiful hearts of women who also live in the heart of My Mother. Listen to, and be nourished by, their love. But the charism of Cor Christi is given by Me, the High Priest, to you as priest, and to all other priests, or priest candidates. Therefore, *be very clear in what I am teaching you. You were allowed the association of women at a very intimate level so I could teach you what you now know.* You will associate more and more with holy laity who will seek to be related with Cor Christi, *but never take spiritual direction from anyone* other than from the priesthood of Melchizedek taught by Me, Jesus, the High Priest. I will also speak to you through Peter, and Associates who are candidates for the priesthood of Melchizedek.

Cor Christi priests and candidates must follow this critical instruction if they and Cor Christi are to succeed. Teach them early in their formation that they can take spiritual direction only from the Trinity, Our Mother Mary, or Mother Teresa while she lives among you. Otherwise spiritual direction must be from My priests.

Through the pain of the last months, in the confusion of voices, you were forced, according to My Father's plan, to be brought to complete abandonment to Me, reaching the full awareness of your poverty. This is why you went back to Calcutta where you first saw your poverty with real clarity, though in a lesser degree. This time you had been so completely torn apart over such a long period, culminating in this last year, 1993, that there was nothing else to rely upon except My Eucharistic Presence lived in My Mother's heart, where you now live.

Mother Teresa's joy over your presence in Calcutta came from *her knowledge that you were now living in full awareness of your total poverty.* This is a true bankruptcy which was needed so that your Lord could take over all that has to be done through you. Peter's share in Calcutta was also in My Father's plan. For in order that he might fully understand Our call in this charism, he had to experience the earthly source of that charism, Mother Teresa's heart.

Many holy laity, including those who were the source of the confused voices, and even religious sisters, will come to this work, and will want to give you spiritual direction. When these situations arise, know that two things are necessary to deal with them: 1) Take whatever they say to those in the priesthood of this work and to your Spiritual Director 2) Let the priests of the work discern whether the advice has any relevance for the work. Have this discernment verified by your Spiritual Director. Then both of you review the advice with Me in prayer, and with each other. *Never let the lay advice stand on its own without priestly consultation. To follow this in complete obedience will eliminate any further confusion of voices.*

Cor Christi, My dear Father George, is the work of My heart, of Jesus Christ, Lord and King and High Priest, for the renewal of this world in the heart of the Trinity. What is to be done is known by no one, and never will be, until it is given from My heart to the priests of the work. To follow any other method will only block, if not reverse, the progress of this beautiful work. From the wisdom of the priest's heart, receiving this work obediently from My heart, will the core of the work be passed on to the laity.

Your abandonment makes it possible for Us to transmit to you the key instructions from the heavenly home where you and Peter are now living in your own beautiful ways. *Never compare yourselves with each other.* You never have, and this is why your love for each other shines to the world in a oneness many find beautiful, but hard to understand. Just live My gifts to you, including the gift of life, in obedience and in your daily "Yes." This is the only thing that qualifies you to be My Mother's children living in My heart which holds yours.

Live now the lessons learned in Calcutta, England, and Rome during this time of travel. I hold you in My love. Pray always in a quiet presence of simple gratitude. We will always receive you in Our embrace.

You are now able to be peace. This is My Father's gift for a new year that will require much interior peace in Our priests throughout the world so that they may be able to withstand the attacks that are coming.

Amen

## 35. PAIN AND JOY IN CO-REDEMPTION
February 18, 1994
Friday after Ash Wednesday
St. Clement's Church
Metairie, Louisiana

*In prayer during exposition of the Blessed Sacrament. Since Ash Wednesday I have suffered intense physical pain.*

Come to Me in your pain and I will tell you of My human life. Every moment of My life on earth was a balance of complete joy and pain. I knew that the salvation of the world would come through the Resurrection. By My suffering during My human life, I understood that I was making amends before the throne of My Father for Adam's sin and the sins of men, who would thus be redeemed. Both salvation and redemption would be offered to My Father in the Resurrection of My Being as Son of God bound forever in unity with a glorified humanity.

You are to live your life as priest in the same model as an offering to the Father—a life of immense personal suffering that will bring immense joy. Your life is a witness to My children that My life, as Jesus and Lord, still continues in the depths of your priesthood for the redemption and salvation of the world. Your witness will be seen not only in your person, but where it essentially shines forth, in the consecration of the Mass, where you and I are completely immersed in each other. On our crosses we unite in a mutual sacrifice at the altar. You, in the bleeding of your cross, lift Me in My Body and Blood, as I am separated on My cross at the altar.

Father George, embrace your suffering. Know that it is meant for the Church and the world, because as priest your suffering is one with My own. This is especially true in regard to the physical agony that our Father sends to you at this time of your priestly life, as well as in the agonies and pains of your heart and mind, through which you share with Me in My Gethsemane experience, which also is yours. It gives an appropriate witness to the priestly birthing of Cor Christi, which is My crucified and resurrected heart.

Without these personal agonies, you will never know, with the degree of intimacy willed by My Father, the meaning of My own bleeding and crucifixion. Only by sharing in this suffering with Me will you know the true magnificence of My Resurrection. Only through the intimacy of both the suffering and the Resurrection, can you then teach the spirituality of Cor Christi, which We have been giving you for three years, to those who will be brought to this way of life.

Those who accept the Cor Christi rule will also experience My agonies and joys, and the agonies and joys of Mary's life as well, as you do. It must be so, for the crucifixion is essential to being a co-redeemer. This is what the Scripture revealed when Simeon told Mary, Our Mother, that her heart would be pierced. Then she could be called co-redeemer. For only those with pierced hearts can, in a sense, baptize into existence new works of My heart and renew lives. In their pierced hearts they have bled water and blood in their being.

Not everyone called to this work undergoes the same degree of suffering, though all are called to be co-redeemers. Cor Christi members are to live lives of co-redemption. Their numbers may not be great, but their suffering and resultant joy will be. These persons, up to now unknown, will be the instruments of the renewal of the world. They will live in the overlay of their crucified hearts in Mary's heart, in My Sacred Heart, and in the heart of My Father. No one has ever been given this exact charism in the Church before, for never before has it been so needed.

You can and must reach out to all Our children with your teaching. Many will follow, especially young men who will come to the priesthood. It is very much a unique part of the plan for Cor Christi that the men with broken hearts will recognize in their call the depth of their brokenness, but also that a true personal resurrection is taking place, which will be realized in the life of Cor Christi. Go forth to renew the world.

With a love that only the Trinity can bestow, I ask you now to rest in peace and live quietly with the patience known to the great saints and mystics of the Church. Many lived in such silence and quietness of heart that no one was able to recognize what was being born in their hearts, minds, and souls until the time came for it to be obvious to all.

I love you, My dear Father George, and I extend that love of My heart to all with you who have heard My call.

Amen

## 36. UNITY OF HEAVEN AND EARTH
March 29, 1994
Tuesday Night of Holy Week
St. Joseph's Abbey
Spencer, Massachusetts

The patterns of life of the two worlds of heaven and earth are meant to overlay each other in a manner that is analogous to the overlay of hearts about which I have been teaching you for three years since 1991, when I first brought you into My heart, wherein you would learn all you must teach from your heart.

Cor Christi is of the hearts. The basic teaching modality of Cor Christi is the exchange of messages of the wisdom of My Father from heart to heart. These messages are received in your contemplative prayer, where your heart is open to receive the anointing, not of oils, but of a learning that bypasses the intellect. For when your heart is open to My Father's heart, the Holy Spirit with your angels will speak to it in the language of infused wisdom. This wisdom can be confirmed by the intellect at a later moment, but it is never learned first by the intellect.

Tonight in the chapel you understood that in the depths of contemplative prayer to which I desire to bring you, you will find layers upon layers upon layers of heavenly choirs praising the life of the Trinity. You first experienced these choirs in the Philippines. You awoke from sleep to find your hand numbering your rosary, bead by bead, with your voice united to endless choirs singing the "Hail Marys," while Mary watched at the foot of your bed with such joy. You realized that your voice was united with the voices of infinity, and yet, with complete clarity of mind, you knew that your lips were not moving. This event was Mary's special invitation to you to be her priest of the rosary, and to live a life that would bring you into union with the choirs of angels and saints. Your experience of that life in such a powerful way will enable you to enkindle in others the desire to partake in such sublimity.

It is nothing you achieved by yourself nor can others achieve it by

themselves. You learned it through a heart open to Mary's presence
and to the voices of heaven in praise of her as Queen of Heaven and
Earth. That night you were allowed to experience the unity of the
Mystical Bodies of the Church, suffering on earth and triumphant in
heaven. Your later experience of Purgatory was a teaching of this additional dimension. In this experience Mary told you that Jesus wanted
you to see a dimension of life distinct from life on earth. It, too, was
a teaching given to you through the openness of your heart.

Tonight in evening prayer you affirmed correctly and clearly that
the first purpose of all life on earth is that it be a life of continual praise
of the Lord, lived on the cross of earthly life, fulfilling what St. Paul said
about carrying out what Christ did not complete on earth (Col. 1:24).

We are providing you with these insights at this time, because
what the world has yet to learn is that the model of the heavenly
choirs of angels in praise, ordered in a grand hierarchy, is the model
from which the world is to discover its own design. The heavenly
choirs have many jobs and duties. You have many jobs and duties or,
if you will, multiple vocations.

Mother Teresa has taught you well, especially in your visit to
Calcutta in January of this year. She has spent a lifetime in teaching
the necessity of an undivided love for Jesus. Yes, your work is born
from the charism My Father gave to her. You, too, must teach the
need for adoring Me in My Eucharistic presence. Mother's audience
is the hungry of the streets. Your audience is the hungry in spirit.
Teach them that their lives here are to be a continual praise of My
Father. As you teach the messages of Cor Christi to leadership, they,
when converted to My heart, will desire their personal and working
world to be a world that is obedient to the Commandments. The
voices of the world are not now a song of praise of thousands of
voices. You saw tonight at evening prayer the voices of the world praising God, not in white robes, but in their families and in their professional situations where their lives are being lived.

When you were first introduced to the reality of your being united
with heaven during moments of time, participating with the heavenly choirs singing the rosary, and at another time participating in

the sufferings of Purgatory, you were confirmed in the realization that one is destined for the beauty of heaven. You firmly acknowledged that no one should even think of desiring Purgatory.

Now, with so much teaching given in Cor Christi to the laity and the priesthood about the absolute need to be Eucharistic in every dimension of one's life, you can understand that you must live in an unqualified obedience to My Father and to His call to each of you. Then you can live on earth loving one another as I have loved you. Father, because it is so essential that you see this, we have given you glimpses of it from time to time during these three years, yet with clarity of sight, hearing, and confirmation. All the dialogues I have given you are like the larger beads of the Our Fathers of the rosary. They elucidate powerful, intermittent, visual understandings on this mystical rosary of knowledge which My Mother hands to you as I speak, and fashion additional beads for you to teach all who are in My heart.

My Mother has often come to earth to call Our children to repentance, to conversion, to prayer, to the Eucharist and to pray the rosary, for these are the basic means by which hearts become open to the hearts of Mary, My Father, and to My own. Then we can fill your hearts with a joy that can only come when you have sacrificed your desires and accepted Our desires, for We know that this is the only way to build a world on earth that praises My Father.

It is My Father's never-ending longing to have heaven and earth united in a great song of praise. Earth's song of praise will be lives lived in the undivided love of My heart. Such lives, whenever they occur on earth, are received in heaven as a great song of loving praise riding upward like waves of incense to My Father's throne.

Cor Christi must recognize the necessity of obedience to My Father. Dispel from people's minds the notion that obedience is a punishment. It is a true *obéissance*. It is the greatest act of love man can give God, and it is the supreme praise of God on earth. No words will ever describe the desire which My Father has to see His creation on earth living in a way that finds its very meaning in the hierarchy of heaven: in the Trinity, in Mary, in the angelic choirs, and in all the

Saints of heaven who are your teachers. Father George, teach my children these realities. Be Cor Christi. Place your heart into Mine. Pray and write and teach, which is also to say: listen, confirm what your heart hears, and bring it to My people through your teaching and your retreats.

Be a holy person and build holy nations. The sign of holiness is joy, and joy is the pedestal from which praise is sung.

The angelic choirs live the life of government which is the model for earth's government, but since My people do not pray, they do not know this model. The Saints do live, and did live the life of praise, obedience, and joy on earth, a life which all My children must know is the correct life on earth.

There is an enormous gap developing between the domains of heaven and earth, growing exponentially each day as Satan convinces My children on earth that there is no God in heaven, that the Eucharist is not My presence, that the priesthood is not needed, and that lives of purity of mind, body, and heart are no longer necessary.

I come to you tonight to urge you to exhort your beautiful members and friends of Cor Christi to evangelize the world so that, while living on earth, you will spend your days looking to heaven and placing your hearts in My Mother's heart and My own. Then We can teach through you the intimacy of the overlay of Our hearts with yours so that you will also come to see the great overlay of heaven upon earth, like blueprints on a drawing board superimposed on one another. All earth is to find its model in life as lived in heaven in all its various layers.

Your obligation as Cor Christi members is to come to Me in prayer. I will be faithful in teaching you what you have to know to do your work. It is central to Cor Christi to pray and listen, to confirm and write, and to teach. Confirmation will always be by the priests.

This Monday of Holy Week one reads the message of Isaiah 42:4: "There will be no justice on earth until the coastlands receive the Lord's teachings." Thus, today, on this Tuesday of Holy Week, I follow yesterday's reading with this teaching to you. This work is very, very serious. The world must be converted and We have asked for this work to be done alongside of Mother Teresa's work and that of many others. None of you can do it alone, but there is great strength in numbers.

Your time in Maine is being given to you at this precious stage of the development of this work so that you will have hours and hours and hours to pray, and listen, and write, so that you and others may be able to teach from the heart of Cor Christi.

Listen with a beautiful and quiet heart during this monastic week. You and I will speak often of this work. This is a most important time for you.

Rest in joy, in love, and in great faith that I am directing you. I love you, My priest. Follow all the directions, counsels, and advice of your Spiritual Director. He acts in My place to challenge you, to love you, to correct you, and to bring you My forgiveness through the absolution of the great Sacrament of Reconciliation, which you have learned to love so much. There is great joy in heaven for those who love this sacrament. He is My priest for you, and again, another model of the overlays of hearts. His holiness, realized through his obedience and through his own great sufferings, is now there to be laid over you, as you, too, are suffering in your own life of abandonment to Me and to the Trinity. When two priests love and share, one with the other, in My name, their love is of Me. Their lives are the very song of praise We desire from all Our children. You are now moving, with My guidance, Father George, into a time that will be characterized by deep prayer and great peace. Cor Christi and My Father's Church on earth will benefit from the fruits of this period. .

Good night for now. You are on the cross, but know always that it was through the cross that I, your Christ, redeemed the world.

Amen

# EPILOGUE

The first set of Father Tracy's dialogues explains the charism, spirituality, and structure of the Cor Christi Institute. The next set, which will be published in the next book, carries its spirituality to a new depth.

The task of the dawning millennium is to bring God's truth to all persons. Many who possess and are guided by rays of this truth are at odds with one another. Leaders who accept God's truth, and in whom it produces an ordered love, will be able to arrange the affairs of the nations and of their cultures in a way that is harmonious, just, and peaceful.

There are three monotheistic religions: the Jewish, Christian, and Mohammedan. These religions teach that there is one, transcendent, loving, merciful, all-wise God, the God of Abraham, Isaac and Jacob, and of Ishmael and Esau. They have in common the Ten Commandments given to Moses, reaffirmed by Jesus, and by Mohammed in the Koran. These commandments enshrine love of God and of neighbor. It is in the observance of these commandments that the peace of the world consists, for through their universal observance all violence and war would be abolished: "they shall beat their swords into plowshares . . . nation shall not lift up sword against nation, neither shall they learn war any more." [Isaiah 2:4-7]

Of course each of these religions has its own specific doctrines, and each is very much misunderstood. Therefore to advance the mutual brotherhood among the men and women of the world, dialogue to clarify these misunderstandings is necessary.

Dialogue does not have as its end the conversion of either party to the faith of the other. It is true that Christians and Muslims believe they have a divine imperative to share their religion with humankind. But this mission and dialogue are separate processes. Dialogue which leads to mutual understanding, friendship, and to the devoted pursuit of God in one's own tradition, as well as to cooperation in redressing the injustices that oppress peoples and individuals, is a worthwhile goal apart from conversion, and one which can help to remedy many of the disorders that abound among us. It should aim at, and lead to, the sincere practice of one's own religion. This is an important goal. Thus Mother Teresa aimed, and the Missionary Sisters of Charity aim, at the practice of love, manifest in the care for those who are needy, for children, and for the dying, regardless of whether they are Hindu, Buddhist, Muslim, or Christian. Likewise, John Cardinal O'Connor in his graduation address at the Hebrew Union College-Jewish Institute of Religion in Manhattan on May 14, 1988 said:

> You contribute nothing to those of us who are Christian, and we contribute nothing to you, if we compromise what is most precious to us...I see too many Jews, as I see too many Christians, caught up in a passion for respectability, in a passion to be 20,000 percent American and therefore not Jewish. This passion consumes, destroys the soul.

He urged the graduates to be true to their tradition of making sacrifices and of suffering for their faith:

> You must teach these words that never disappear. You must teach these words of the Talmud, these words of the Torah.

Christianity has its foundation in Judaism, and this must be remembered. As the Cardinal said on this occasion: "Catholicism owes its life-blood to Judaism." He added that as an archbishop it is his duty to teach that no one who is anti-Semitic can be a true Catholic.

There is a *particularistic* component in Judaism. It is *this* people of *this* land who were chosen by God for a special mission. This is acknowledged by the New Testament and the Koran. But there is also a *universalistic* component in Judaism. To Abraham was given the promise that in his seed all the nations would be blessed (Genesis 22:18). Such universalistic sentiments also abound in the psalms and in the prophetical writings.

Jesus, presented in the New Testament as the Emmanuel, that is God-with-us, reasserts the binding character of the Ten Commandments as expressions of the love of God and of neighbor, and He stresses the interior dispositions from which actions in accordance with the Ten Commandments arise. Thus He says, "not what goes into the mouth defiles a man, but what comes out of the mouth, this defiles a man." (Matt.15:11 RSV), and, "You have heard that it was said, 'You shall not commit adultery.' But I say to you that every one who looks at a woman lustfully has already committed adultery with her in his heart. (Matt. 5:27 RSV).

As the Catechism of the Catholic Church says [581 and 1968], Jesus as God could reinterpret the moral law, the Ten Commandments, deepening them in accordance with their inner dynamism, yet without altering them. Jesus, by allowing Himself to be crucified, fulfilled the prophecies, for example, of the Suffering Servant of Isaiah, and the cultic law, which offered animal sacrifices, seen by Christians as prefiguring the sacrifice of Christ, He Himself being "the lamb of God," as St. John the Baptist called Him. Thus both the moral law and the cultic law intrinsic to the Torah were fulfilled without the loss of an iota. In this way the particularistic elements of the divine revelation given to Israel were superseded by the universalistic elements of that revelation, making it available to all peoples of all times.

The basic clash, then, at the trial of Jesus was the question of His exercising divine authority. Of course this issue still separates Christians and Jews. Yet the Catechism of the Catholic Church teaches [430, 433, 616] that Jesus' redemption of the Cross was not a separation, but a reconciliation of all persons to the one God of Israel, salvation coming from the Jews, as Jesus said to the Samaritan woman at the well (John 4:22).

Jews will be better dialogue partners if respect is shown to their sensitivities, which result from centuries of discrimination and persecution by Christians. Similarly the dialogue between the Orthodox Christians and Catholics must take into account sensitivities arising from their mutual history, including the sack of Constantinople by the Crusaders in the twelfth century. Just as the Jews are the elder brothers and sisters of Christians, so all Christians in virtue of their baptism and faith in the Messiah whom they believe to be the Prince of Peace and the Emmanuel prophesied by Isaiah, are brothers and sisters. All persons are children of God.

In particular, the Orthodox autocephalous Churches share with the Catholic Church almost everything except the Pope and the development of doctrine. They have apostolic bishops, the successors of the founders of original sees of the Church, they have sacraments, they have a priesthood and celebration of the Eucharist that the Catholic Church recognizes as valid, and they have a rich spirituality and monastic tradition. John Paul II says that with their reunion, the Church will breathe with two lungs!

These statements are in accord with what the Directory on Ecumenism of the Secretariat for Promoting Christian Unity of May 14, 1967 says:

> 40) Between the Catholic Church and the Eastern Churches separated from us there is still a very close communion in matters of faith (cf. Decree on Ecumenism n. 44); moreover, "through the celebration of the Eucharist of the Lord in each of these Churches, the Church of God is built up and grows in stature. And, although separated from us, yet these Churches possess true sacraments, above all by apostolic succession, the priesthood and the Eucharist . . . " (ibid. n. 15).

Muslims, increasing in number in the West as the West's indigenous population diminishes, must not be confused with the extremists among them. Muslims have a tradition of prayer to the same God that Jews and Christians worship. They have a strict moral code stemming from the Ten Commandments which they accept as inspired. They acknowledge Abraham, Moses, the Prophets and Jesus as one of the prophets, and have a devotion to His Mother Mary.

Father Tracy's Cor Christi Institute stems from Mother Teresa's charism, as she has testified, and as his autobiographical chapters make clear. And for Mother Teresa, every human being was sacred (including the unborn), to be respected, loved, and assisted. At the time when Albania was the most atheistic Communist country, banning all religious expression, its President told her that it was against the law to establish there a religious community. Nevertheless she prevailed and brought in more than one of her communities of sisters, who were enthusiastically welcomed by the people. Eventually the Catholic Cathedral was opened. Mother Teresa was not satisfied, however, until a mosque was established for the Muslims, who constitute a majority of the population.

Dialogue should lead to mutual love. Rabbi Baruch Goldman, rabbi emeritus of the congregation Beth El of Worcester, a holocaust survivor, who lost his entire family in the Shoah, said to eighth graders at St. Mary's school, Shrewsbury on February 11, 1998, that God created all people and he asked why a Jew should say he is better than a Christian or a Christian say he was better than a Moslem. He said that he believes in a God who heals and provides and that there is goodness in each person, although some "tore out their longing for goodness."

And Cardinal O'Connor, speaking at a luncheon sponsored by the national executive committee of the Anti-Defamation League in Palm Beach in February 1998 asked, "Can we learn to really love one another enough even to disagree with one another?" He added that love is the next logical step for Catholics and Jews.

While the Cor Christi Institute recognizes, together with the great religions, that all human beings are children of God and that all should love one another, it has a more specific task, mentioned in the Preface and set forth in the dialogues. It intends to further the renewal of the Church, which had a great impetus in the second Vatican Council, and particularly to foster a renewal of the ordained priesthood, which will teach the laity to recognize their royal priesthood and together build a holy nation at the service of all peoples.

Cor Christi aims to facilitate the recognition by everyone that peace and fulfillment lie in the awareness of, and response to, the presence of the Lord in the Eucharist and in the tabernacle. Anyone of any faith, as experience shows, can enter a Catholic Church and sit there for fifteen minutes, enjoying peace and coming away with a renewed perspective. Youth especially need to realize that there is a purpose which gives meaning to the emptiness, alienation, and suffering of their lives. Cor Christi hopes to give youth that help.

Each of these initiatives for the improvement of society has its own distinct value. Dialogue overcomes emotional prejudices, fosters friendships, and often leads to a deepening of the participants observance of their own tradition. A natural, but distinct, consequence is cooperation of persons of different traditions in building a religious, moral, and truly free society.

Beyond the dialogue, cooperation, mutual respect, and love of all persons, Cor Christi desires to put a renewed Catholic Church, priesthood, and laity at the service of society in the acknowledgment of the fatherhood of God, the presence of His Son in the Eucharist and tabernacle, the Commandments, and His tender, solicitous care for each person, and of the consequent brotherhood of peoples. Cor Christi hopes to bring leaders to this realization, so that they can cooperate in building a civilization of love.

# INDEX

## Symbols

104 Bellevue Avenue, 38

## A

A.B., 49
Abdo, Michael, 52
Abortion, 131, 132, 164, 172
  great, caused by My priests, 132
  of a perverted priesthood, 132
A.R.C.I.C. (Anglican-Roman Catholic
  International Commission, 51
abandonment, 164, 167, 184, 185, 193
  *see also detachment*
  feelings of, and of meaninglessness, 180
  sacrificial, and depth of prayer, 164
Abraham, 22, 194, 195
academia, 49
Achacosa, 66
Adams, Edith Clark, 35 *see also Clark*
advanced education, 44
advice, woman's, 183
Afable family, 66
affluence, 14, 21
agenda, without, 163
Agnone, Dr. Frank, 76
agony, 182, 186
Albania, 197
America looks to self, 161
  cultural problems, 160
  is in deep spiritual trouble, 161
American
  approach, 161
  appointee, 51
  Church, 124
  solution, 158
  ways, 161
angel(s), 101, 121, 132, 166, 177. 189
  *see Gabriel*
  and saints, choirs of, union with, 189
  choirs, 192
  the fall of, 168
Anti-Defamation League, 198
Antiphon Psalm, 119, 156
apostasy, time of, 139
applicants for priesthood in the Cor
  Christi way, 165
Araneta, 66

apostasy, time of, 139
applicants for Chor Christi priesthood, 165
Aranata, 66
Argentina, 154
Armstrong, Chantal, 81
ashram of Father Bede Griffiths, 52
Associate Member(s), 122, 158, 175
Assumption Abbey, 13
attachments, 182
attack, 113, 114, 157
authentic teaching, 24
autobiographical chapters, 15
autonomy of the social, political, and
  economic orders, 22

## B

Babendrier, Father Joseph, of Opus Dei, 61
Bal Harbor, 34, 35
bankrupt, spiritually, 56
baptism, 23
  of desire, fire, or water, 139
  of water, desire, or fire, 168
Barry, Hugh, 82
baseball, 28
basic formation, 158
bearer of hate, 131
beauty of creation, 41
Becksted, Mary Ann, 76
beginning of the Cor Christi Trinitatis
        Institute, 64
Bellevue Avenue, 27, 29 *see also 104*
Bellevue Stratford Hotel, 52
  Ballroom, 52
Becket, St. Thomas, 37, 79
Benedictine ashram of Father Bede
  Griffiths, 52
Berkeley Hundred, 38
Berryville, Virginia, 52
Beth El, 198
Bibby, Elizabeth, 84
Bilderbergers, 151
Bishop, 51, 61
  of Portland, 14
  Vogel, 52
Blessed Sacrament, 24
Body and Blood, act of consuming, 131
Boothbay summer visits, 42
Boston College, 49

## INQUIRIES

All inquiries regarding the work described in this publication should be addressed to Rev. Msgr. George E. Tracy, Ph.D., at one of the following locations:

## ADDRESSES

### COR CHRISTI TRINITATIS INSTITUTE

**NORTH AMERICA**

11 Bangor Mall Blvd. Suite D373
Bangor, ME 94401
U.S.A.

**UK/EUROPE**

65 Eaton Square
London SW1W9BQ
England